LIVE,
LEARN,
LEAD

A Lifelong Journey of Leadership and Purpose

JOAN A. ZANDERS

Live, Learn, Lead
A Lifelong Journey of Leadership and Purpose

Imprint: JA Zanders LLC

ISBN: 979-8-218-78550-5 (Hardcover)
ISBN: 979-8-218-78551-2 (Paperback)

Book Design by Transcendent Publishing
Editing by Mary Rembert

DEDICATION

Since I don't know if there will ever be a second book, this dedication will be lengthy:

- To my family—our children, grandchildren, great-grandchildren, and my siblings and their families, who fill my heart with love and joy and who challenge me daily to make a difference in this world

- To my NOVA Financial Aid staff, the "best of the best," who exuded professionalism and expertise and made my job and life rewarding beyond belief

- To all the excellent role models, including but not limited to my parents, grandparents, aunts, uncles, cousins, teachers, administrators, friends, and colleagues from multiple professions— ALL whose leadership skills and examples I have observed and learned from throughout the years

- To those in leadership roles who showed me what NOT to do and be as a leader (Nothing serves so well as a bad example.)

TABLE OF CONTENTS

PROLOGUE

Over the past several years, friends and colleagues have encouraged me to write a book. My response to each was always, "About what?"

No one could verbalize the plan. My mind spewed forth a plethora of options from biographical to novel. Doris Kearns Goodwin, Bob Woodward, and David Grann are all incredible writers. I love historic fiction and have always wished I had the patience and inclination to research an era adequately and write a storyline like James Michener, Diana Gabaldon, or Ken Follett—or like Tony Hillerman, Sara Donati, Mark Twain, or Joseph M. Marshall III, who expose readers to both history and native cultures. I am confident that will never be my genre, no matter how I wish it to be so.

In September 2022, Sam, a friend and former work colleague, came from Virginia to visit me in Iowa. As we were talking one evening, he said, "You should write a book!"

Again, I asked, "About what?"

He thought for just a few seconds and responded, "About leadership and professional development!"

That gave me pause. Though I have had a raft of experiences and leadership opportunities—and have presented on various related topics many times throughout my 34 years in higher education as a Director of Financial Aid—I never once considered leadership and professional development as a book topic for me. It sounded egotistical! I then responded, "What if no one buys it?"

Sam quickly said, "That doesn't matter. You are writing it to share your knowledge in hopes that it will help someone else. You aren't writing a book to make money."

Not long thereafter, I mentioned the possibility of a book to Kendra, another trusted friend and colleague, and wondered about the sensibility of it. She immediately said, "I would read it! But I also love to hear your stories!" When I told her Sam's idea, Kendra said without hesitation, "Life and leadership."

Within a few days, I started outlining thoughts and units that could be included in a book. To my surprise, my presentations throughout the years contributed. Not long thereafter, Billy Ray, another friend and former colleague, said, "Think about the decades of your life and all the gender challenges you have hurdled too." Indeed! Ignoring that aspect would yield an incomplete and inaccurate picture.

This is NOT a textbook! Throughout this book, the "life" portion of the story has resulted in the inclusion of anecdotal experiences that hopefully demonstrate what led to this book.

I have no delusions that my offering will become the next bestseller, but I hope you find the book entertaining, that some piece of this work will resonate with you, and that you might grow in some small way from reading it. I certainly did from living it!

Preliminary Information and Career Timeline for Perspective

By profession, I am an educator, with over 34+ years of experience as a Director of Financial Aid, serving in four-year private, four-year public, and two community colleges during that time. Hiring well, training staff within and outside financial aid, collaborating across the institution, providing exemplary customer service, and maintaining compliance have always been essential components of my leadership within each financial aid operation where I have served.

I have held leadership roles at the state, regional, and national levels, and have presented, facilitated, and trained at all levels numerous times. Though each of those roles provided opportunities for continued growth, they are not the focus of this book.

My profession and avocation have focused on my father's advice to make the world a better place for having been here. Both of my biological parents were lifelong educators. I believe education can be the great equalizer if offered with quality and resources for all at all levels. Providing financial assistance for students who might otherwise not attend college and assisting students to program completion are reflections of that passion.

I offer the following abbreviated work history to provide perspective, though this "epistle" is about far more than financial aid leadership:

January 2022 through October 2024

Upon retirement from Northern Virginia Community College (NOVA) at the close of business on August 31, 2021, I was immediately asked to provide consulting assistance for other colleges and universities, addressing a plethora of needs. The goal of my consulting work was to support university financial aid operations in their efforts to assist students while maintaining compliance and providing exemplary customer service. I worked as JA Zanders, LLC, during this time.

June 2008 – August 31, 2021

I served as Director of Financial Aid for Northern Virginia Community College, a six-campus community college just outside Washington, D.C., with enrollment of approximately 76,000 credit students at the time of my retirement, including students from over 180 countries.

From March 2019 to March 2020, I served as Interim AVP for Enrollment Services at NOVA with supervisory responsibility for the Office of Financial Aid, the Office of Military and Veteran Services, and the College Records Office.

While at NOVA, I was responsible for a complete restructuring of Financial Aid, which centralized the department and transformed NOVA Financial Aid into a department that students respected and valued, and other departments wanted to emulate.

I worked closely with all Provosts and Vice Presidents to support and solve problems and served on many committees, including, but not limited to: Substantive Change; Credit for Prior Learning; NOVA-Mason ADVANCE Leadership Committee; College-Wide Diversity, Equity, and Inclusion Committee; and many Virginia Community College System (VCCS) and State Council for Higher Education (SCHEV) workgroups.

2007-2008

High School Outreach Specialist for EducationQuest Foundation, Lincoln, Nebraska

1997-2007

Director of Financial Aid, Northeast Community College, Norfolk, Nebraska

<u>1991-1997</u>

Director of Financial Aid, Wayne State College, Wayne, Nebraska

<u>1987-1991</u>

Director of Financial Aid, Nebraska Christian College, Norfolk, Nebraska

<u>Prior to 1987</u>

Substitute teacher while our children were young

Church high school choir and handbell choir director

Agent with Northwestern Mutual Insurance Company

If you have ever questioned whether your story matters or wondered if your path could lead others forward, I invite you to walk with me through the pages ahead. I hope you will find encouragement, connection, and perhaps a few leadership lessons that resonate within your own life.

CHAPTER ONE

"LIFE IS WHAT HAPPENS WHILE WE ARE MAKING OTHER PLANS"

Life is too short to learn everything by experience. How many times have I said that to our children, especially during their teen years! I also prayed every night that they would make good choices and acquire a bit of wisdom before they permanently hurt themselves!

There were moments, but in case you are wondering, yes, they did. Get wisdom that is! Nothing is more rewarding to a parent than to see one's children grow into caring, contributing, compassionate adults—and parents!

We are each the sum of our experiences—experiential learning, formal education, reading, watching, and absorbing from those who influence our lives. Life experiences become a part of who we are. My experiences are not yours and vice versa, even if we experienced a life-changing event at the same exact time—together! We take in and interpret new information based on our past experiences and socialization. Not all learning experiences are positive or in our best interest, but we can still learn from them. On occasion, we must "unlearn."

I tend to be a big picture person and often think about cause and effect. Much of it is forward-thinking. I haven't determined if it is a gift or a curse. When participating in meetings where major decisions are being made, it baffles me when participants can't see what will happen in the future if a particular option is chosen.

Looking backward, I always contemplate how we got from Point A to Point B, whether as an organization, business, or individual. For some reason, in an attempt to reach Point C, I feel the need to learn from experience, the path from A to B, regardless of whether the path was positive or negative, and not to make the same mistakes again. I in no way claim to have all the wisdom, but it baffles me when I see individuals in high-level positions make decisions that are so contrary to long-term progress or the greater good.

Some years ago, while I was also Director of Financial Aid, I felt an urgency to create and teach a college sociology class at night, entitled "Issues of Unity and Diversity." We met one night a week for three hours, which gave us ample time for in-depth discussion and experiential learning.

I had three classrooms, one in front of me and two over interactive cameras at distant locations, which we would now call distance or remote learning. My class tended to fill with more than the average number of adult students. One of them called me some weeks after the class had ended to ask if she had permission to use one of our class exercises with her business colleagues. Perfect … pay it forward!

I feel strongly that we can't know where we are going if we don't know where we have been. When we have a better understanding of what makes us who we are today, we can choose whether that is the person we want to be in the future.

It is not always easy, but each of us can unlearn inaccurate and prejudicial thoughts and behavior by acquiring accurate information. I encouraged students to discuss, learn, and grow.

As a first assignment, I asked class members to research their personal histories. Some knew much of their families' backgrounds, but others really had to search by talking to their parents, grandparents, and great-grandparents. Most were surprised by what they learned but were grateful for the learning, even if parts of their histories were difficult. In class presentations, each student was told to share only the history they were comfortable sharing.

Since I ask it of others, I must also be open to sharing. What follows is a snapshot, not an autobiography, and stories are intertwined throughout the book. As so accurately stated by Allen Saunders and John Lennon, "Life is what happens while you are busy making other plans."

CHAPTER TWO

MY FIRST ASSIGNMENT, TOO

I begin my story with the singular event that influenced my life more than any other, my mother's death from cancer a month and a half after my seventh birthday. Mom went into the hospital the day after my birthday and came home once before being transferred to a larger hospital in Omaha.

I still have a vivid picture in my mind of Mom sitting on the divan in the dining room with a cup of tea. Her hands were shaking so badly that she could hardly drink the tea. I also remember being called into the living room with my siblings about 9:00 a.m. on a Sunday morning in early February, and Dad breaking the news that Mom had died.

As I recall, we went to church that morning. A girl a year older than I asked me if my mom had died. I never forgave her for that—for making it real. I spent the next few days with my friend Pam and her family about a half-block from our house, while family members and friends came and went from our house.

I also have a clear mental picture of being in the sanctuary of our church and seeing Mom in her casket. Until I talked about that quite recently with my older sister, I thought I might have imagined it, but I didn't.

Until I was an adult, I couldn't talk about my mom without crying. In that era, or in my family, the thinking was that talking about it caused more pain, which instead gave no outlet for pain that was already so deep and real.

It was also 1952, the middle of the Korean War, and a few short years after WWII—with more than enough grief to go around. Until I was an adult and my aunt shared more details with me, I didn't know Mom had cancer. All I heard was yellow jaundice. The news articles (and even the death certificate) said a blood clot in the heart, which was the "actual" cause of death. In the early 1950s, I also think there was a stigma about cancer. So little was known—and seemingly, still is.

I was the middle child of five, all about two years apart, and under the age of 10 when Mom died a short month and a half after we were aware she was ill. The original diagnosis was yellow jaundice, which I now realize was a symptom, not the disease. Visiting her in the hospital in Omaha is still a vivid picture in my mind. I took pictures to her that were made by my whole first-grade class, and I still remember what I made: a raised vase on construction paper filled with cut-out flowers.

Mom had tubes everywhere. One was giving her blood. When she had a blood clot, my young mind thought they had just given her too much blood. In reality, my uncle had been present in the surgery a week before her death, which was not mentioned at the time, when the surgeon found advanced cancer in her liver. Whether the cancer was a primary or secondary cancer that originated elsewhere, we will never know. The blood clot shortened her life by a week or so and probably saved her from more pain.

My two sisters were older; my two brothers were younger. Our dad was the school superintendent in a small town in southwest Iowa. We went through two to three housekeepers before Dad remarried.

One of the housekeepers was a peculiar woman from the hills of Missouri. I went home with her one weekend and remember sleeping on a featherbed over the top of creaking springs. My sisters started calling me the "go-go girl" because any time going someplace was mentioned, I was ready. (Still am, by the way!)

Our stepmother was younger than Dad by 11 years and a struggling widow with a daughter and two sons, who age-wise just happened to fall into three of our two-year slots, with our stepsister being the oldest and the boys just older and younger than I. When Dad and our stepmother married, there were eight children under 11 years of age.

I'm pretty sure my stepmom had no idea what she was getting herself into. She told her younger sister, an aunt for whom I babysat one summer and with whom I became quite close, to stay out of it; she was moving up in this world—because of Dad's position, I guess. It felt like she spent the remainder of her life trying to prove herself.

Even though she adopted us, and Dad adopted my stepsister and stepbrothers, we were never referred to by Mom as "our children." We were "my children and Orin's children." My personal relationship with my stepmother was rather like a roller coaster—sometimes fun and supportive, sometimes rocky, distant, and painful. Our stepmom's later years were quite bitter and impacted by dementia.

My biological mother had been an English teacher and had started on her master's at a time when most women didn't even go to college. Mom was the oldest and the only girl in a family of six children.

Mom's great-grandparents came from Sweden in the late 1800s and homesteaded in northeast Nebraska on a timber grant, which required planting a certain number of trees per acre of land. Until recently, I didn't realize that homesteading on timber grants and Arbor Day are actually connected.

While touring Arbor Lodge, the home of Arbor Day founder J. Sterling Morton in Nebraska City, not far from my home in southwest Iowa, I learned that the first Arbor Day in the United States was April 10, 1872. Over a million trees were planted on that first Arbor Day.

The Timber Culture Act of 1873 was a follow-up to the Homestead Act of 1862 and offered an additional 160 acres of land to homesteaders if they agreed to plant a portion with trees, originally 40 acres but later reduced to 10. Tree planting was encouraged to provide resources like fuel and building materials, and to act as windbreaks on the treeless prairie.

My maternal great-grandfather opened a family store in Royal, their small community in northeast Nebraska. Seventy-five years later, when the roof caved in from heavy snow, the store—and products therein, from thread boxes to button hooks—looked the same as they had in the early days. Pictures through the years were identical, with the exception that the tree in front had grown.

One of my uncles, the youngest in the family, once told me that my mom had basically raised him while Grandma was busy with the other children. Mom was very loving, but was reportedly not a good housekeeper, though I don't remember that. With five young children, who had time to keep the house sparkling clean?

Another aunt told me Mom always said, "My children won't remember if the house is spotless, but they will remember if I took time to read them a story." My stepmom did not go to college and, in my mind, tried to show she was better by insisting on a spotless house.

We girls cleaned the house every Wednesday and Saturday! I can remember being down on my hands and knees, paste-waxing and polishing the hardwood floor around the edge of the carpet at the new house at least twice a year. Granted, eight kids did tend to create a lot of dust and clutter!

No doubt, my stepmother had plenty to do. The constant focus on cleaning the house most likely led to my sister's response many years later, when on a phone call, I told her I'd better get off the phone and get the house cleaned. Her response was simply, "Why?" Hmmm … good question!

Needless to say, life was challenging. Dad was well-respected in the community, and we had a terrific educational experience in our small community. Dad hired great teachers, coaches, music directors, and everything else! Several actually came from the area where Dad grew up. Though I don't remember ever being pressured to excel, striving for excellence was just understood. My next-older sister recently asked me if I remembered what Dad used to say, which I didn't.

"Good, better, best—never let it rest—until your good is better and your better is best."

Most of us participated in every extracurricular activity we could—I perhaps more than the others. Practically speaking, in a small school, if we didn't participate in a lot of activities, they probably wouldn't have existed! In a recent conversation with my next-younger brother, I mentioned that I didn't remember ever fighting with my siblings, with one exception. To that, my brother replied, "Because you were never home!" That thought had not crossed my mind.

Dad was extremely busy but spent every minute outside his time at school working in our huge garden (we ALL did!), raising milk cows, chickens, rabbits, steers, hogs—anything that could help feed a family of 10. We lived in town, though no part of the country was more than six blocks in any direction!

One hot summer day, I went down to milk the cow. The shed was unbearable, so I tied her to a tree and sat on the stool to proceed with the milking. The process seemed to be working, but I apparently was not very good or fast enough at the task. After a few minutes, "Bessy" got tired of the whole process and simply walked around the tree, leaving me sitting there. There is a lesson in there somewhere!

During one period, probably pre-television, Dad read to us in the evening, often a chapter or two at a time. Two books I remember well were *Little Britches* and *Brighty of the Grand Canyon*.

Perhaps influenced by my mother, who was an English teacher, books and reading were always very important in our family. I remember well receiving a book of my own for a birthday present, *Secret in the Old Attic*, a Nancy Drew mystery. I still have it and several books that were my mother's, now my "prized possessions."

Growing up in the Midwest meant cold, snowy winters, hot, humid summers, and often extreme weather. Tornado warnings were common. I stood in our driveway when I was a young teenager and watched clouds that were ugly green and boiling. That night, tornadoes hit all around our town and totally wiped out my friend's farm, most of a small town east of ours, and the farm of another girl I knew from a neighboring town west of us.

A second storm I recall was a torrential downpour and flash flood north of us. We missed the downpour but were asked to stand on the bridge overlooking the East Nishnabotna River as the water moved in our direction to watch for bodies; several people had been swept away. We saw the bodies of cows, pigs, and horses float by, but thankfully, no people. I wasn't very old, and the images are firmly imprinted in my mind.

In the spring and fall, the Missouri River flyway becomes the route for thousands of ducks and geese. My dad and brothers were hunters, but my memories include short trips with my dad to just watch the huge flocks of birds in areas like Forney's Lake and the Riverton bottom, where the East and West Nishnabotna Rivers begin to converge. While admiring the ducks and geese, we couldn't hear ourselves talk; the incredibly vociferous birds numbered in the thousands.

The Riverton bottom is also prone to flooding. Another memory is of my dad gigging fish in a flooded ditch where they were trapped, and Dad getting stuck in the mud and having to swim out of his hip waders while we small children watched helplessly!

Forney's Lake is now dry, and I am told the DNR has no funds to run pumps, which could provide water back onto the land. Watching the migrating waterfowl now on the sandpit lakes just north of my community is so peaceful and a reminder that "The more things change, the more they stay the same."

At one time or another, our family delivered every one of the five newspapers that came to the community. I delivered the *Shenandoah Sentinel* for several years.

We could ride down every street in town and tell you who lived where and which dogs to avoid. My brother does that to this day! I could also tell you where every household struggled to pay and sometimes owed weeks at a time when I was collecting, which was part of the job.

In the summertime, we girls played softball with our school team, and the boys played Pee Wee or Midget baseball. The boys—not all or at all times—later played high school baseball, football, and basketball, and ran track. My brother's relay team still holds the state record after many years. It lasted for several years and was then etched permanently in the record book when yards were changed to meters! We girls, some more than others, participated in all sports as well.

On Sunday afternoons (no field lights), we watched our dad play first base for town team baseball until he was 50! Through baseball and other sports, my dad knew my future husband, his dad, and brothers, who were all talented baseball competitors from a neighboring town. Two of his brothers later played in the Yankee organization. The Yankee "connection" led to an unexpected and amazing conversation some years later when my husband ran into Billy Martin and Elston Howard in a hotel bar and restaurant in Milwaukee.

My future husband, who was six years older than I, actually coached against me as an assistant coach in softball and basketball when he taught in two different schools in our conference. It never occurred to me that I would one day date and marry someone as "old" as a coach!

As the Superintendent, Dad coached girls' basketball and took several teams to the state tournament, but quit coaching when his daughters started high school basketball. He didn't think it was fair that he would be our coach, but he was always one of three voices I could hear from the stands—my coach, Mr. Plummer; the boys' coach, Mr. Hackett; and my dad. Both Mr. Hackett and Mr. Plummer were later inducted into the Iowa Coaches Hall of Fame due to their successes over many years of coaching in our community.

I loved sports! My first basketball game against another town was as a player on the fourth, fifth, and sixth-grade team when I was in fourth grade. In my senior year, we made it to the quarterfinals of the state tournament.

At that time, Iowa was one of two states that even had girls' interscholastic athletics. All schools were in one class, though most of the large schools didn't have girls' sports as yet. Girls' basketball was a six-player sport, with three forwards on one end, opposite three guards from the opposing team, and three guards on the other, defending against the opponent's forwards. Players couldn't cross center court. The game was one with a lot of screening and finesse. No three-point line existed, and high-percentage shots were encouraged.

My two older sisters were forwards, but my oldest sister had graduated, and my stepsister was no longer playing by the time I got to high school. Though not exceptionally tall by today's standards, I was post forward.

Until she graduated after my sophomore year, my next-older sister was a guard. When she effectively defended the opponent's best scorers, few people even noticed her limp from polio, which she survived at age five.

Growing up, my sister, the guard, was my "defender" too. At one point, she and I argued about something neither of us remembers—probably her attempt to guide me in the right direction, and I didn't speak to her for three days, the one exception to no "fights" with siblings. Nothing hurt her more at the time, and I regret that to this day. Conflict-resolution skills came much later for me.

My siblings and I grew up without the benefit of vaccines, other than the vaccine for smallpox. Other vaccines had not been developed yet. I remember three-day measles, German measles, mumps, chicken pox—we had them all! At least one time, we were quarantined at home, and the owners of the grocery store dropped off groceries and left them on the front step, keeping a running total, as usual, until the end of the month.

My two sisters and I all had our tonsils removed in the hospital at the same time. And I added scarlet fever and rheumatic fever to my health history and got quite used to having vials of blood drawn from my arm. It hurt less if I watched—and still does.

Several years after my sister recovered from polio, the whole family drove four hours to see my uncle, a doctor, to get our Salk vaccine shots, and later, we took the Sabin vaccine on sugar cubes.

In addition to fast-pitch softball (I was the pitcher) and basketball, I ran track for a few years (missing a hurdle and landing on the cinder track was a deterrent!) until the boys' coach started golf. Our closest golf course was Shenandoah, so we learned how to hit golf balls in a pasture on Stony Point, a big hill north of town.

I used my dad's clubs, which included an adjustable iron with a pretty heavy head. Though now illegal, I wish I still had that unique club, a collectible and conversation piece, to be sure. The guys chasing me with a five- to six-foot-long bull snake could easily have resulted in that club becoming a weapon!

After I married, my husband became a golf pro for a few years before going back to school administration, and I played a lot of golf. I even played in a state tournament in Nebraska and later co-chaired the Iowa Women's State Golf Tournament when we lived in Storm Lake.

Golf remained a lifelong part of our family, with children and grand-children taking up the game. At one point, when I was quizzing our little two-year-old grandson on what animals lived where, he suddenly asked, "Grandpa live at the golf course?" Out of the mouths of babes . . .

When I got to college, the only choice for sports was intramural bas-ketball. My initial college was in Missouri, but we recruited a group of Iowa girls with basketball experience and won the league. As a rule, colleges didn't have interscholastic women's sports, though I did get a recruitment letter from AIB in Des Moines and one from the Texas Cowgirls, a team that traveled like the Harlem Globetrotters and actu-ally played men's teams. My folks provided a definitive "NO"!

Our school had extremely strong music programs and small groups. I was an alto in choir and sextet and played the saxophone, from alto to tenor to baritone. I also acted in several plays and even directed a one-act play in my senior year.

Each one of these activities provided an opportunity to work with a team, and on many occasions, to lead. Though I didn't really think about this at the time, the carryover skills were significant. Although the academics of school are critical to future success, I would encour-age any student to get involved in extracurricular activities. Possibilities exist for everyone, and the benefits are far greater than scores, the win/ loss column, rankings, or what one can add to a college application, though I must admit to realizing this long after high school.

During my senior year, in addition to singing in our girls' sextet, our choir director encouraged me to take a solo to state contest. I did well, still remember the song, "Prayer Perfect" from the poem by James Whitcomb Riley, but mostly remember that my knees were shaking so badly that I'm not sure how I walked back to my seat afterward.

I don't remember those nerves ever again to that extent, and sometimes think I should be nervous when presenting when I'm not. For me, at least, the more I did it, the more comfortable it felt, another benefit of extra-curricular activities, and, of course, preparation.

While in high school, I was also asked to sing a verse for part of a choir anthem at church. The verse was from "Brighten the Corner Where You Are," a song made popular by Ella Fitzgerald. I am truly not a soloist and have no illusions that I sang it like she did. The lyrics from both songs spoke to me then and still speak to me these decades later.

Prayer Perfect

Dear Lord! Kind Lord! Gracious Lord! I pray …
Thou wilt look on all I love tenderly today.
Weed their hearts of weariness; scatter every care.
Down a wake of angel wings winnowing the air.

Bring unto the sorrowing all release from pain;
Let the lips of laughter overflow again;
And with all the needy, O divide, I pray …
Thou wilt look on all I love tenderly today.

The verse I sang from "Brighten the Corner" was this one, which is followed here by the chorus:

Here for all your talent you may surely find a need,
Here reflect the bright and Morning Star.
Even from your humble hand the Bread of Life may feed.
Brighten the corner where you are.

Brighten the corner where you are.
Brighten the corner where you are.
Someone far from harbor you may guide across the bar.
Brighten the corner where you are.

I spoke at my high school graduation. Strangely, I wasn't as nervous speaking to that gymnasium full of parents, siblings, relatives, and students as I was singing solos. I was prepared, but I also had more confidence in my speaking voice than my singing voice.

Our class motto was, "We have crossed the bay; the ocean lies before us." We were, after all, the Admirals! In my "speech," I used the analogy of the river. (No, I did *not* claim it was an original thought, I do not know or remember what prompted me to use it, and, yes, general references to people were, in *proper* English of the time, always masculine!)

"When a man puts his hand in a river, the water downstream represents the past, the water upstream the future, and the water that he touches is the present … never to be relived but never to be forgotten. Such is the river of life."

Somewhat fortuitously, I quite recently read something similar in a book. In Wally Lamb's *I Know This Much Is True*, copyrighted 35 years later, Dr. Patel, one of the characters, says, "Life is not a series of isolated ponds and puddles; life is this river you see below, before you. It flows from the past through the present on its way to the future. That is not something I have always understood; it is something I have come to a gradual understanding of through my work as both an anthropologist and a psychologist. 'Life is a river,' she repeated. Only in the most literal sense are we born on the day we leave our mother's womb. In the larger, truer sense, we are born of the past—connected to its fluidity, both genetically and experientially."[1]

---

[1] Wallis Lamb, *I Know This Much Is True* (London: Harper Collins, 2000), p. 610.

So many lessons in this river of life analogy. The past is gone … learn from it and file it. The future is yet to be experienced … opportunity … adventure … the unknown … plan for it. The present is fleeting…don't waste it.

As Russell Baker writes in his memoir *Growing Up*, "We all come from the past, and children ought to know what it was that went into their making, to know that life is a braided cord of humanity stretching up from time long gone, and that it cannot be defined by the span of a single journey from diaper to shroud."[2]

Perhaps because of my mother's death when I was so young, I learned and clung to the importance of family, the journeys my ancestors had taken, and the realization that none of us is an island unto ourselves. The realization was comforting, while simultaneously a dictate to make a difference.

Each summer, my sisters and I helped pick, can, or freeze dozens and dozens of quart jars of tomatoes, green beans, corn, applesauce, raspberries, strawberries, beet and cucumber pickles, and even meat on occasion. We butchered chickens and rabbits for the freezer. At one time, we had over a hundred breeding does. Imagine the bunnies!

One year, Dad bought a hundred-plus old red laying hens—cheap—to clean for roasting. We spent hours picking out pinfeathers, sometimes using tweezers. Skinning them was not an option. We detasseled corn for seed corn companies that were creating hybrids, walked bean fields for farmers to cut out weeds and corn that grew voluntarily from remnants of last year's crop, babysat for numerous families, and even cleaned a huge chicken house for a farmer. I can still smell the ammonia and dead chickens. Don't get me started on that one!

Corn detasseling was in crews of workers, same sex, as I recall, though our crew boss was male. Detasseling usually began in June at the

---

[2] Wallis Lamb, *I Know This Much Is True* (London: Harper Collins, 2000), p. 899.

time, though it would likely be much earlier now, and could last for several weeks.

One long year on the job, the area had heavy spring rains. The tassels don't wait! We walked through yucky, mossy water up to our hips to get into one field over on the Sidney bottom. I swear the mosquitoes grew to the size of hummingbirds that summer, and the heat and humidity made the loose pollen stick to the skin and itch like crazy!

Other years weren't as bad. Detasseling was also a social time with friends. I learned the hand jive dance at the end of the corn row from my friend Darlene, who learned it while watching Dick Clark's *American Bandstand*.

On one incredulous day in the bean field near the old drive-in theater, one of my friends who was working on our bean crew was rushed to the doctor after the corn knife he was using, which he casually dropped to the ground, bounced up, and cut him on the shin. Five stitches later, he came back to give us the results.

While he was gone, my little brother picked up the corn knife to see if it had blood on it, as a kid would do. When he returned it to the ground, it popped up and sliced another of our group across the top of her foot. I still have the scar from those three stitches.

Dad always had a major project for us in the summer, as well. I realized much later that one of Dad's goals might have been to keep us busy and out of trouble! We bought and remodeled a house to sell, which became known as the Little Pink House.

On the land behind that house, we planted rows and rows of potatoes. We had so many potatoes when we dug them in the fall that we filled a flatbed trailer; then, we stored them in gunny sacks in a vegetable cave at my stepmom's cousin's farm. Imagine our disappointment and nausea when we found the potatoes were spoiling! That required sorting and pitching a great many of them. If you've never smelled rotten potatoes, you're really missing out! I remember picking up potatoes and my fingers going through them.

We tore down a big two-story house and then built our new house on the property when we outgrew our original house fairly quickly after Dad and our stepmom married. An elderly lady had lived for years in the house we tore down and had a shed full of interesting old items. I wish we had kept more of them, or at least had more time to sort.

In the house, my brother even found a beautiful, 14-inch, scalloped-edge knife with a looped handle that was between the studs inside the plaster and lath walls. I still have it and wish it could talk because I'm sure it has a story to tell.

The men who built our new house teased me incessantly. Though I was blond and skinny as a rail, a man named Freddie called me the Little Red-Headed Fat Girl. He also sent me to the lumber yard to get a left-handed monkey wrench and, another time, a skyhook. Humor at my expense!

The school purchased land across the street south of the school to add outdoor tennis and basketball courts and playgrounds. On the corner of the property was a little cottage that looked like part of a fairytale. I looked forward to each visit with the elderly owners, Mr. and Mrs. Evans. Until they passed away, leaving the cottage empty, they never had a refrigerator, just an icebox.

The house was surrounded by plants, flowers, and trees of all varieties, and a clothesline with little wren houses on each end. Four huge oak trees lined the west side of the property. The squirrels loved the acorns, but we loved to use them to make little people!

Mr. and Mrs. Evan's house was not salvageable, and our family tore it down after the school purchased the property. We were working on tearing it down in 1957 when my older sister came down to tell us that our maternal grandpa had died suddenly of a heart attack.

It's amazing how impactful moments are remembered so vividly. Grandpa was a strong, handsome man—the picture of health. As he did every morning, he got up early, dressed, and gently slapped Grandma on the hip, saying, "Time to get up, Ma!" But this morning, he did all that and then fell over her and died.

When the bond issue passed for a new school addition to alleviate over-crowding, our family tore down a huge church on the same property south of the school that had been used for several years as extra school classrooms after the church closed. My husband-to-be was fortunately tied on when he fell through the roof of that cathedral ceiling! He must have really been trying to impress my dad!

Most likely influenced by the Great Depression of the '30s, Dad saved everything! We pulled nails out of the lath, bundled the lath to sell, and straightened all the nails to be used again. In the old houses we tore down, most had square nails. I also remember being on my hands and knees with a blowtorch in the heat of early August, removing asbestos tile from the floor of the old science lab in the church and trying to save them! Some were saved, but so much for "friable" … most of those tiles were fried!

Until quite recently, I thought little of it, but we must have been the "go-to" family for hired help. The boys had numerous haying jobs every summer, and we girls babysat constantly. I couldn't have been more than in fifth grade when I first babysat small children.

The summer after my junior year, I babysat four boys (mostly the youngest two, since one of the four was older than I and one two years younger), cleaned house, washed laundry, and cooked for them all summer for $15 per week. I even remember driving the two youngest to swimming lessons in Shenandoah, the closest pool.

The boys were all good kids, and the experience was worthwhile, additional preparation for what a woman "was supposed to do" at the time. By the way, no one is a better project manager than a full-time housewife/homemaker, though the "wages" certainly didn't and still don't reflect the ability or requirements of the job.

Some years later, work done as children became a talking point while waiting for a performance to begin at the Kennedy Center during my time living and working in Virginia. The colleague who invited me grew up in southern Virginia, which might have influenced the conversation.

I shared some of my experiences and asked her if she had ever done anything like that. She quickly responded, "White children didn't do that kind of work." That comment will forever be imprinted on my mind, and, quite honestly, whether fair or not, changed my impression of her.

At a board meeting of the Virginia Association of Student Financial Aid Administrators, which I scheduled that year at Carter Hall, a beautiful historic mansion on the western side of Virginia, a similar discussion ensued. While relaxing after dinner, we discussed our ideal jobs and then the worst jobs we ever had.

When I mentioned detasseling corn, someone said, "Corn has tassels?" When I mentioned walking beans, the response was, "Why would you walk beans?" Even though these were not all "city slickers," I realized they were also not raised on or near a farm, or didn't have to do the work. I began envisioning beans on leashes.

Though I don't remember being excited about some of the jobs I had, the work ethic I developed has served me well. And I have been told by more than one individual in different parts of the country—and in a Johnny Carson recording—that Midwest residents are known and valued for their work ethic.

Hard work was a necessity in a large family, and the skills learned then carried over to adult life. I cooked and baked quite a lot. Sounds far-fetched, but the cast-iron skillet we used was about 18" across to accommodate four frying chickens at a time. I was so used to cooking for a large family that my husband gained 20 pounds during the first six months we were married. I didn't want many leftovers!

When my husband became the golf pro at a club in northeast Nebraska shortly after we married, I offered to fix breakfast for the golfers on Sunday mornings. Each ordered what they wanted, and I prepared it … it didn't seem challenging.

I sewed or purchased my own clothes from at least the time I was in junior high. The exceptions were the beautiful hand-me-downs we got from our affluent cousins in California, which were a treat and provided us with stylish choices we didn't see in Iowa. One year for Junior-Senior Prom, I wore a floor-length, off-the-shoulder, fuchsia satin gown that had been my cousin's. I felt like a princess!

Hand-me-downs from cousins or my older sisters were the norm and truly appreciated. Sewing became the practical way for me to have cute clothes for myself and for our children later on, and I started "designing" some that I couldn't buy.

My most complicated project was a wool plaid suit jacket with so much matching—complete with padding stitching on the lapels—that I made for my husband. Unfortunately, I was almost done with it before I decided it was too long. Big mistake! Yes, we often learn more from our mistakes than from our successes.

A recent realization was that sewing, gardening, and cooking were among my first attempts at project management—not the scope of the millions of dollars later financial aid projects would entail, but good lessons. Starting with an idea was the first step. Developing that idea then became a combination of creativity, logic, and reality. Whether it be a piece of empty land, a large uncut swath of material, or a hungry family, the project launched. Taking the pieces of a complicated pattern, cutting them correctly from the material, and figuring out how to effectively put them together into a finished product, sometimes without a pattern, was a lesson in project management. Getting from point A to point B smoothly required envisioning the final product and took patience and commitment, especially when the instructions were not always easily understood or complete.

Gardening is much the same, but the ultimate "project" is raising children. Those who have good role models can do their best to mirror that model. Not all would-be parents have had such models, which is why parenting classes can benefit children, parents, and society.

Some projects provide a clean blank slate and good examples from which to build and learn. Others require one to "build" from the ground up, remove real or figurative weeds and debris, till the earth, decide what to "plant," plan what goes where, and fight off the vermin, water, hoe, and weed before ever realizing the results, figuratively or literally. Sewing, gardening, cooking, and raising children were all great lessons in project management. To mix metaphors yet again, sometimes you hit a home run!

CHAPTER THREE

CHALLENGES FOR WOMEN

Growing up in the 1950s and 1960s was a dichotomy! The '50s were the *Leave It to Beaver* years when most mothers were not working outside the home—not necessarily by choice.

Commercials had women vacuuming in their dresses and heels. Then the '60s came with Haight-Ashbury and the birth of the counterculture movement—essentially opposition to most of the social norms valued by previous generations (i.e., our parents and grandparents).

The 1950s me would not have dared wear a miniskirt. Small town, mid-America U.S.A., for the most part, was a bit out of the loop and months behind the west and east coasts, though I do remember well a student sit-in at my college in the early '60s that blocked a major U.S. highway for hours, a protest over food in the cafeteria that resulted in the director being fired.

I was a student employee for her eccentric husband in the student services office and didn't consider participating. Breakfast eggs were fried hours ahead, and the food, in general, was not great, but I tended to lean toward my dad's response when he was asked after an out-of-home dining experience if the food was good. "I didn't know they made any other!"

When I graduated from high school, the choices for women were rather limited beyond marrying and becoming a housewife. Most women who chose careers became secretaries, beauticians, nurses, teachers, or airline hostesses—not that there is anything wrong with any of those professions. I wanted to be a doctor, but I knew of no women doctors.

"Though the percentage of medical doctors who are female is increasing steadily (38% in 2022 compared to 26% in 2004 according to the AAMC), the AAMC reports that almost 40% of women physicians go part-time (30.6% for females compared to 4.6% for males) or leave the profession altogether within six years of completing their residencies. Gender harassment, salary inequity, gender bias, and work-family conflict seem to be the primary reasons."[3]

Both my personal physician and my uncle, who was a doctor, dissuaded me from becoming a physician. The response was, "But you want to be a mother, don't you?"

My uncle at least seriously considered the possibilities and suggested I become an anesthesiologist. He thought I could stay in the medical field, but I would have better control of my schedule. Putting people to sleep all day did not remotely appeal to me.

Though I didn't like killing anything and still don't, having cleaned all manner of animals, I was not at all squeamish about blood or internal organs and was thinking more along the lines of a heart or brain surgeon. I wanted to find solutions, likely influenced by my mother's early death.

I was one of a few females in my graduating class who immediately went on to college. Some went to beauty school, while others attended

---

[3] Amy Paturel et al., "Why Women Leave Medicine," AAMC, October 1, 2019, https://www. aamc.org/news/why-women-leave-medicine.

secretarial school. I recently had a conversation with a dear lifelong friend. She went to Iowa State and majored in home economics because that is what she knew. She fairly quickly changed her major to the science field, though that was certainly not common at the time.

My dad never made me feel like I was limited in what I could do, though I knew without asking that paying for college would be my responsibility. Dad would co-sign a loan, but the burden was on me.

I had taken four years of French in high school, taught by one of my favorite teachers, and chose French, the language of diplomacy, as my major and Spanish as a minor, thinking that if I couldn't be a doctor, I could become a UN interpreter. My parents were a little opposed to my venturing that far away. (They struggled with my going to Omaha on a date, much less to New York City.)

It never occurred to me not to go to and finish college. Even when my dad introduced me to my future husband at the Iowa Girls' State Basketball Tournament my freshman year of college, and we married during my sophomore year, I never once considered not finishing college, though NYC was now off the table.

I transferred twice to schools closest to my husband's work and still finished in three and a half years, taking heavy loads and attending summers while picking up new required classes at my new school. I had far more than the required 120 credits when I graduated. In that era, I never lost even one credit through transfer, which doesn't always happen today.

Fighting the Good Fight

The women in my family were women before their time. How could I NOT go to college?! My maternal grandmother graduated from Wayne Normal School in 1908 and gave the valedictory address. I still have a copy of it. My mother was an English teacher who had earned her bachelor's degree and had begun work on her master's degree at Greeley State Teachers' College in Colorado in the summer of 1938, at a tough time in history and a time when few women even went to college.

My dad's older sister and her husband both became teachers and signed contracts in Colorado. When they arrived, they realized they would have separate schools on different mountains, where they could be snowed in—and apart—for weeks and possibly months at a time. Not what newlyweds wanted! They loaded up again and drove to California, where timing and wise investments in real estate made them quite affluent.

Growing up in a small town, I didn't realize that I must have been pretty naïve. As my husband and I prepared to marry, I felt it was a good idea to have my annual physical and ask the doctor some questions that were weighing on me. I didn't know anything about a "climax" or if this should happen regularly. When I talked to the doctor in my college community, he took it upon himself to "demonstrate" the concept by massaging my breasts.

I quickly said I understood, vacated the premises, and never went back. For some reason, magnified by embarrassment, I didn't feel I could tell anyone. It would have been his word against mine, and I was pretty sure I knew how that would end. I just wish I had known self-defense and could have used a well-placed knee. Though most professionals would never do such a thing, it does happen, and I hope women today have the strength and courage to speak up. Until very recently, I had never shared this experience with anyone.

For many years, between the late 1800s and the mid-1940s, when bans were widely lifted after WWII, married women were not allowed to teach in many areas of the country. A woman providing her own income when her husband was considered her support was taking a job from a man. A "married woman's place" was in the home, after all, and God forbid she should be pregnant and working with children!

During WWII, women were *needed* outside the home and consequently *allowed* in many previously denied areas of work. My mother's sister-in-law and her sister traveled to California to become "Rosie the Riveters."

Though Title VII of the Civil Rights Act of 1964 outlawed discrimination in employment based on sex, income levels are not always equal to this day. I was quite oblivious to all of this and never dreamed that I would earn less than a man for doing the same job, though I still remember hearing comments from outside my family that the best way to hang on to a woman was to keep her barefoot and pregnant, which likely meant no job. Perhaps hearing that made me even more committed to having my own income and, consequently, choices.

I really wish I had talked with my grandmother about her views on the 19th Amendment and how she felt when she was finally able to vote after the 36th state ratified the amendment and it was certified on August 26, 1920. Grandma would have been 31 at the time—my mother almost eight.

Wyoming was the first state to support women's suffrage, which happened in 1890. Western living being what it was, their women were needed. Colorado followed in 1893. (One of the slogans from the opposition was "Giving the vote to women will increase the irresponsible vote.") Utah and Idaho approved in 1896, but no other states did so for 14 years.

Title IX, which was enacted as part of the Higher Education Amendments of 1972 and to this day prohibits sex-based discrimination in any school or other education program that receives federal funding, wasn't passed until nine years after I graduated from high school.

As I understand it, Title IX was initially more about access to postsecondary education than with athletics at the college level. Since men were the breadwinners, open spots for college students were previously prioritized for men, which subsequently pushed women toward marriage or into lower-paying jobs. Title IX has recently been "rewritten" and is currently tied up in the court system. Current executive orders on non-discrimination could further impact Title IX.

Even with gradual improvements for women in the workplace, some factors weigh heavily on a woman's opportunity for advancement. Though children are born of two parents, mothers still bear primary responsibility for childcare, which is both a blessing beyond measure and a challenge.

Years of preparation and possible advancement in a career can be lost if mothers leave their professions to bear full responsibility for childcare. Why is childcare not an equal responsibility for both parents, which would then balance the impact and also provide children with care from parents instead of childcare providers? If childcare providers are required, why are we as a culture not more committed to providing quality childcare and good-paying jobs to those providers?

In January 2025, Gallup released the results of a poll on bearing the cost of children, and listed childcare issues as one of seven challenges the workplace would face in the coming year.

The data from Gallup showed that working women (38%) and men (37%) in the U.S. are similarly likely to strongly agree that their organization provides them with the flexibility needed to address childcare responsibilities. But working women with children are significantly more likely than men to consider reducing their hours (44% vs. 24%), decline or delay a promotion (35% vs.18%), or consider leaving their job (38% vs. 15%) due to childcare issues or family obligations.

At one college where I worked, a childcare center was hosted on campus and available to students and staff alike for drop-in hours. Those using the facility were not obligated to pay for full-time childcare if they needed fewer hours of care for their children. Not only could parents see their children during work or class time breaks, but students training in early childhood education had the opportunity for paid internship-type job training right at the school.

What if more companies, including colleges, offered childcare for staff and students? What a benefit for parents and children! Though opportunities for women have increased through the years, some areas of concern that seem solvable continue to hold us back.

Opportunities for women and girls to compete in athletics were quite limited across the country until recent decades. Smaller schools in Iowa have had intercollegiate basketball for women since 1920.

In 1925, when the Iowa High School Athletic Association decided it was harmful for girls to engage in "strenuous" activities such as basketball, they voted to no longer support girls' basketball as a state-sponsored activity. At that point, 25 men from primarily small rural Iowa school districts formed their own organization, the Iowa Girls High School Athletic Union, so that girls could continue playing basketball and eventually other sports.

When I was in high school, Iowa was still one of only two states in the nation with girls' high school athletics. As I recall, Tennessee was the second. My dad coached three high school girls' basketball teams to the State Tournament in the 1950s, but gave up coaching when my oldest sister got to high school. He didn't think it was fair for him to coach his own daughters, and he surely understood how challenging it was for each of us to prove that we deserved whatever opportunities we got when he was already the Superintendent, much less our coach.

After giving up coaching, Dad was very active in the Iowa Girls' High School Athletic Union (IGHSAU) and served as President at one point. During those years, I was able to go with him to Board meetings at Templar Park in Spirit Lake, Iowa.

During one of the IGHSAU Board meetings, I tape-recorded interviews with each board member on the value of girls' high school athletics. I took the recordings to the head of Nebraska's Athletic (or Activities) Association, who happened to be at the college I was attending in Nebraska. He listened intently and then suggested maybe intramurals or possibly volleyball, which, unlike today, was "gentle," slow, and a bit like watching paint dry. Nonetheless, the seed was planted.

Having shared a small gymnasium with boys' teams and physical education classes for years, it had not occurred to me that guys in some larger schools viewed a gain for girls as a loss for themselves.

Later, when I was a substitute teacher at a larger school in northern Iowa that still had no intercollegiate athletics for girls, I broached the subject of girls' athletics in a chemistry or physics class of mostly young men that I taught for a few days. The response I recall so well from the guys was, "What?! And give up *our* gym time?!" My immediate unspoken reaction was, "How very selfish of you!"

Within a year or two, girls in all schools in both states had intercollegiate sports at the high school level. The evolution of girls' basketball included teams with a "rover," which my aunt played in long-ago decades, to six-player with three forwards on one end and three guards on the other, to five-player, similar in many ways to the game played by young men.

The Iowa Girls' State Basketball Tournament, held in March each year, celebrated its 100th anniversary in 2019 and was—and still is—a huge event with lots of color, entertainment, and single-elimination games that pit Iowa's Sweet 16 against one another until a state high school championship team is crowned.

When I was there, we all played in one class. Now, teams are classed by school size, making competition more equitable. A whole museum exists in Des Moines to celebrate "The Iowa Girl."

Softball and track were also common sports for women, but neither had the magnitude of basketball. I feel very fortunate to have grown up in Iowa and to have had the opportunity to participate in state-wide athletic competition.

I'm not taking credit for the acceptance of athletics for women across the country. I was just another voice screaming in the dark. Like athletics for men, athletics for women develop teamwork, personal growth, leadership skills, physical and mental acuity, and so much more. How we have grown!

In 2023, Iowa State University women won the Big 12 Basketball Tournament. Earlier the same week, the University of Iowa women won the Big 10. To have both win in the same year was incredible. Fortunately, both finals were televised.

On August 30, 2023, I watched the University of Nebraska Huskers of Lincoln, Nebraska, beat the University of Nebraska Mavericks of Omaha, Nebraska, in three volleyball sets at Memorial Stadium *football* complex in Lincoln. Attendance for the event was 92,003, a world record for any women's sporting event ever! Watching the Huskers and so many other women's teams play volleyball with so much skill is truly fun and exciting, nothing like the backyard sport of 60 years ago.

On October 15, 2023, the Iowa Hawkeyes women's basketball team hosted DePaul before 55,646 people at Kinnick (football) Stadium in Iowa City, another record attendance.

In February, University of Iowa star Caitlin Clark, a graduate of Des Moines Dowling High School, set the all-time women's scoring total. Now, she has surpassed the scoring record for both women and men in NCAA history, has broken countless other records, and continues to do so at the WNBA level for the Indiana Fever. We've come a long way, baby!

As I was recently checking out of a beautiful hotel in Santa Fe, an older Latino gentleman working as a valet asked me where I was from. When

I said Iowa, he said, "Do you know Caitlin Clark?" Unfortunately, I do not. He went on to tell me how much he admired her for what she has brought to women's basketball and added to greet and thank her for him if I ever met her. What an influence she has had!

A terrific historical read on how little freedom women had 150 years ago can be accessed in *The Woman They Could Not Silence* by Kate Moore. Set in Illinois, this true story tells the experience of a minister's wife who disagreed with her husband's fire-and-brimstone teaching and, unfortunately for her, bravely shared her views in a Bible study class. This mother of several small children was then removed from her children and home and institutionalized by her husband in an insane asylum in Illinois.

Her fight for freedom over two plus years and the deceitful behavior of the institution's administrator create a snapshot of our country's history of marginalizing half of the population by gender—and numerous other people groups—since our founding. I also recommend a wonderful book of "fiction"—or not—by Bonnie Garmus, *Lessons in Chemistry.*

My maiden name was Mann. Once on a staff outing, an autumn and proverbial "three-hour boat tour" on the Potomac, when we were each sharing something no one in the group knew about us, and another time at an all-school reunion when my class members were honored as the 50-year class, I stated that I used to be a Mann.

What was heard by my staff and by many at the reunion was "man." The looks on people's faces told volumes about their beliefs. At the school reunion, a third of the audience laughed because they knew me and the fact that Mr. Mann, my dad, had been the superintendent at Farragut for 20+ years in the 1940s, '50s, and '60s. Another third would no longer look at me or make eye contact. The last third were likely thinking, *That explains a lot!*

That singular statement with each group has been handed back to me on countless occasions over the years, often by people who weren't even in attendance. Understanding and acceptance of LGBTQ+ individuals had a long way to go then, and though improving, still does based on the current political environment.

In 2025, Gallup research data shows that 68% of Americans say same-sex marriages should be legally valid, while 64% view same-sex relations as morally acceptable. In 2001, only 38% of respondents indicated that same-sex relationships should be valid, and 40% thought same-sex relationships were morally acceptable.

From this data, the trend shows rising support for same-sex marriage and acceptance of same-sex relations over the past two decades, but both measures have edged down slightly since peaking in 2022.

According to Gallup, "The declines are driven largely by shifting views among Republicans: In 2022, 56% said same-sex relations were morally acceptable, compared with 38% this year. Support for legal recognition of same-sex marriage among Republicans has also fallen, from 55% to 41% over the same period."[4]

"Walk a mile in their moccasins" before you abuse, criticize, and accuse seems most appropriate here. Being the judge and jury for another person is way above my pay scale.

I recently pulled a book off my bookshelf that I had purchased some time ago and never read, Mark Twain's *Joan of Arc*, originally copyrighted in 1896 and 1899. Much of the history within the book is a translation by Jean Francois Alden of "Ancient French into Modern English from the Original Unpublished Manuscript in the National

---

[4] Megan Brenan, "Record Party Divide 10 Years after Same-Sex Marriage Ruling," Gallup. com, June 4, 2025, https://news.gallup.com/poll/691139/record-party-divide-years-sex-marriage-ruling.aspx?utm_source=gallup_brand&utm_medium=email&utm_campaign=front_page_2_june_06102025&utm_term=information&utm_content=image_imagelink_1.

Archives of France." Ancient because Joan of Arc lived in the early 1400s. The wit of Mark Twain is generously interwoven within history and makes the book very entertaining, as well as informative.

When the yet uncrowned King of France finally supplied Joan with an army, the priests then expressed grave doubts as to whether "the Church ought to permit a female soldier to dress like a man." The verdict came from two of the greatest scholars and theologians of the time, one of whom had been the Chancellor of the University of Paris.

"They decided that since Joan 'must do the work of a man and soldier, it is just and legitimate that her apparel should conform to the situation.'" Unbelievable! The "Church's authority to dress as a man!"[5]

That section brought back memories. When I was in high school and played basketball in the 1960s, girls did not wear slacks to school or school events. In September 2024, I received this Gallup post from their archives:

Gallup Vault: Shedding Societal Constraints on Women's Attire

1948: Americans' Approval of Women Wearing Slacks at Home and in Public

Do you approve or disapprove of women of any age wearing slacks in public, that is, for example, while shopping? What about wearing them in the home?

	% Approve	% Disapprove
Slacks at home	65	11
Slacks in public	32	44

Response categories "not sure" or "indifferent" are not shown.
Jan. 2-7, 1948

GALLUP

---

[5] Mark Twain, *Mark Twain, Joan of Arc* (San Francisco: Ignatius Press, 1989), p. 141.

Even while playing ball in the 1960s, girls boarded the bus in skirts, nylon hose (with seams, no less!), and dress shoes, only to change into uniforms to play. When I first started playing, uniforms were satin, short, knife-pleated skirts over satin "briefs" and midriff tops—quite a contrast to our required daily wardrobes.

The first uniforms we had in junior high were silver gray and fuchsia, hand-me-downs from the high school team; the next were blue-and-white skirts and midriff tops, our school colors. Later uniforms were more like those worn today. One of the teams we played had spaghetti-strap midriff tops. The boys sat in the balcony.

Whenever I see the challenges women face in other countries, I realize that the same was true in the U.S. just a few decades ago. One such example from the inner island of Jamaica reinforced this observation.

Though my husband and other male chaperones accompanied me on several of the mission trips I developed and led, I always drove on the trips where a 15-passenger van could be utilized. On one such occasion in the mountains of Jamaica, where driving on steep, narrow roads required one to begin honking on every curve to let possible oncoming vehicles know the road was taken, we stopped for the night at our residence and were greeted by the woman who cared for the property.

She looked at me in amazement and asked, "You were driving?" It had not occurred to me that women in Jamaica, at least in the inner island, didn't do that, especially three plus decades ago with a man in the vehicle.

Driving in Jamaica was an experience, to say the least. Our 15-passenger van was a straight stick, and driving on the left side of the road meant I was seated on the right and shifting with my left hand. At one point in steep terrain, I asked the male chaperone seated next to me to shift the gears when I told him to.

An even greater challenge was avoiding the goats and various other livestock that frequented the roadsides, or the custom of not observing no-passing zones. Forever imprinted in my mind is the image of driving up a steep hill on the left side of a two-lane highway with two other cars to my right—all going up the hill! Prayer was a necessity!

On our first trip to Uganda to work with the Aids Orphans Education Trust (AOET), a student and good friend from Uganda put me in touch with his family, who miraculously lived a short distance from the AOET site, and also with his brother, who was a member of parliament.

I had dinner at the home of my friend's wife and three young daughters. His wife had land and was growing trees to replenish the supply of charcoal used for cooking and to sell to others. Their three daughters were all in school and have since graduated from college with impressive careers.

I am pretty sure my friend, who has recently returned to Uganda, stayed in the U.S. long enough to complete his master's degree, teach, and make money to buy additional land and send his children to college. While he was in the States, his wife was the sole parent and businesswoman.

On that first trip, my friend's brother, the legislator, picked up my husband and me and took us out through his entire constituency area (and later to the parliament building, where bullet holes were evident from past violence).

At one of the villages, the women treated us to a banquet-type lunch and performed a skit for us on preventing mother-to-child transmission of AIDS, which was a major focus in the country at that time.

After the skit, I talked with the women about their challenges. What became apparent was that prostitution was a significant cause of the spread of HIV/AIDS. Both single and married men frequented houses of prostitution. The women said they talked and talked with their husbands, and the husbands assured them they understood. Then the women said, "But at night, they forget all that."

Preventing Mother to Child Transmission of Aids
(skit by village women) plus a group picture

Part of our group visited Parliament with James, my friend's brother.

Another student and dear friend from Malawi came to my office one day, almost in tears. When I inquired about her angst, she shared that her niece had just become engaged. I thought they didn't like her choice in men. Instead, I was told that it mattered little. With HIV/AIDS so prevalent—and no deterrent or medication in sight at the time, marriage would be a death sentence for the niece. An otherwise joyous occasion was, instead, heart-wrenching.

In so many developing nations, women are still subordinate. One could say that is still true in many respects here in the United States. The playing field and incomes between men and women are still not level. The current political environment and the reversal of Roe v. Wade combine to put women in situations where they cannot control their own bodies or ultimately support more children.

Our granddaughter, a social worker, was—until a short time ago—one of the managers for a very large women's shelter, which unfortunately is always full. One woman came in desperate to get an abortion. She had three children under age four and was pregnant again. Her husband controlled her birth control pills. I don't think anyone really loves the idea of abortion—I never have, but I have begun asking myself whether it is kinder to eliminate an embryo before it has knowledge or to allow a birth when the child is neither wanted nor supported psychologically or financially.

Add to that the pregnancies from rape or incest, babies that will be born with terminal conditions, or pregnancies that risk the mother's life or health. Even though making a baby is not a solo activity, the woman still bears the brunt of the work, both before and after the birth. An unwanted child born into poverty will face a lifetime of challenges. It seems that a significant percentage of our population is adamantly opposed to abortion, but conveniently forgets about caring for children after they are born. Social services and support are inadequate to help low-income parents, especially single women, raise healthy, well-adjusted children. We grow our own problems.

The goal of the women's shelter is to provide safe, emergency housing and food and to assist women in finding jobs and more permanent housing outside the shelter. Many have small children ... one room at the shelter will accommodate a family of seven.

Many of the women have restraining orders against their abusers. On more than one occasion, former residents with restraining orders—that seem about as effective as the paper on which they are written—had those restraining orders violated. The result was the death of the woman, and, on at least one occasion, suicide by the man, leaving a small child an orphan.

One of my dear friends and former staff members made the decision to become a social worker after her aunt was beaten and left for dead in the middle of a country road. My friend needed to make a difference. I know abuse is not limited to that perpetrated against females, but women and children certainly experience the preponderance of abuse.

After graduating from college with a degree in communications, the same granddaughter took a good-paying job that she quickly disliked. She resorted back to nannying for a military family while she decided what career to pursue. The family included two small boys, and a third was born a few months into her job. The father was a helicopter pilot, and the mother was a nurse supervisor at the base hospital.

One evening, our granddaughter received a call from the father asking our granddaughter if she could possibly spend the night with the little boys. The mother was in the hospital, and they wouldn't be able to come home. Our granddaughter thought there had been a shooting, but that had not been the case. The mother had told her supervisor on numerous occasions that she was concerned about one of the civilian employees reporting to her. He was bullying and threatening her. The mother had documented all of it, but her supervisor was discounting it all. On the last visit with the supervisor, the mother had been told to bring her supervisor evidence, not emotions.

That evening, after work, when almost no one else was around, the problem staff member came into the mother's office, threw gasoline on her, and set her on fire. He then tried to cut her with a blade or pair of scissors. Had two women not come by, a nurse who smothered the flames and a petite doctor who jumped on the perpetrator's back and somehow subdued him, the mother would not have lived.

Our granddaughter stayed with the boys for months and even drove them from Kansas to San Antonio so they could walk to the burn hospital each day to see their mom. The boys didn't recognize her at first.

Five years ago, when the mother and our granddaughter provided a session on workplace violence at our regional financial aid conference for me, the mother had already had over 200 surgeries. More would be ongoing due to scar tissue buildup, which restricts movement.

The perpetrator was sentenced to 20 years, the maximum allowed by law. The mother could not sue the military for negligence due to laws protecting the military, which by rights should pertain to conflict zones, not civilian-type settings.

How unbelievably amazing and sad that the perpetrator got 20 years, and she got life. And my granddaughter? She recently completed her master's in social work and accepted the position of Director of Youth Services for three homes accommodating 16 to 24-year-olds aging out of the foster care system. What a strong, caring, young woman! I might be a tad prejudiced, but our family is not lacking in strong, caring women—nor strong, caring men, for that matter.

In a recent phone conversation with a dear friend and former colleague, she brought up the topic of male and female energies. She said something that took me by surprise and gave me pause.

She said I was the only woman she knew who had male and female energies in balance, in harmony, and who easily and naturally moved between the two, depending on the circumstances. I had seriously never thought about my personality in that way, but would likely attribute that characteristic to my upbringing.

I was never pigeonholed, especially by my father, to believe my gender would limit what I could do in life, though societal norms indicated otherwise. My brothers never cleaned the house, but my sisters and I did all manner of so-called "men's work" as we were growing up.

We had positive male and female role models, as well, and learned to be simultaneously strong and empathic. I know of no women any stronger than my sisters, and I witness those same characteristics in each of our children. My friend called it a natural "presence"… without saying a word.

CHAPTER FOUR

BUILDING A
STRENGTHS-BASED CULTURE

I nput—Achiever—Learner—Intellection—Maximizer

While I was at Northern Virginia Community College my last 13 years as a Financial Aid Director, I invited a friend of my older daughter, Lori Stohs of Lori Stohs Consulting Group, to spend a day working with our staff on their strengths.

The entire staff, and any subsequent new staff, completed Clifton-Strengths Finder assessments. I began to see greater self-confidence in staff and more appreciation for co-workers when we better understood each other and began focusing on our talents and developing them into strengths instead of not understanding differences, finding fault, and focusing on weaknesses.

I then felt compelled to spend personal resources to complete Gallup-Certified Strengths Coach training in DC so that I could become a CliftonStrengths Coach and continue to work with staff to develop our individual and group strengths. Individuals in the DC training were paired up and provided feedback to their partners at the end of the workshop. I was blessed with the following from my partner:

<u>Joan Zanders</u>
Input
Achiever
Learner
Intellection
Maximizer

<u>Happy to be Me</u>

Standing on the riverside
Possibilities abound, the gap so wide
Thinking, musing what could be
Wondering, wondering—who'll come with me.

Scanning the bank for ways to cross
Searching, searching, at a loss
Thinking, musing what could be
Wondering, wondering—who'll come with me.

Gathering those close to share my path
Unifying, challenging to cross that gap
Discovering possibilities on the other side
Travel with me this gap so wide.

Merging our talents to find a way
Building a bridge will save the day
Discovering possibilities on the other side
Travel with me this gap so wide.

Working together, we build it fast
Crossing the river to future from past
Discovering new worlds, oh so bright
Come with me to do what's right.

Turning around, happy to see
Those closest, following me

Discovering new worlds, oh so bright
Come with me to do what's right.

I smiled, fulfilled
Happy to be Me.

After Strengths Training in NOVA Financial Aid became public knowledge, other administrators at the college asked me to work with their staff members as well, both while I was at NOVA and after I retired. I am told that NOVA now has a Gallup-Certified Strengths Coach in HR who can work with staff members on building a strengths-based institution.

Our "next door" regional four-year public institution, George Mason University, is now all-in with a number of Gallup-Certified Strengths Coaches. I recently told Lori that she had no idea the extent of her influence from that initial day of training, a lesson for all of us.

A common question has been, "What are the best CliftonStrengths that leaders need?" Per Gallup, if you are a leader, *your* strengths are the best strengths for *you* to lead. There are no "top leadership strengths" that are better than others.

In one women's group I was leading, a long-time and very successful state legislator was astounded that "Influencing" was nowhere in her top five. In reviewing with her, she realized that her dominant theme of Relationship Building had helped her successfully work with others to make change. She didn't need "Influencing" strengths to get the work done. Another retired member of the group immediately said, "I wish I had known this when I was younger!"

I have often felt that "Strengths Finder" would more appropriately be called "Talent Finder." Talents are more or less innate qualities that don't become strengths without knowledge and practice to develop them into skills and strengths.

A former staff member asked me if he should concentrate on his top five or his bottom five. My response was that the bottom five are of no importance unless they are getting in your way.

Regardless of what your lesser strengths are, and irrespective of the domain from which you lead, your dominant strengths give you what you need to lead successfully. Individuals with different strengths can utilize their unique qualities to achieve the same goals, which is one reason why Strengths results should not be the sole influence in hiring decisions.

Having said that, individuals will be more successful and happier if they can spend the majority of their work hours working within their strengths—to do what they do best. Specific domains and strengths tend to better support some professions and responsibilities more than others.

Per Gallup, examples include the following:

Strategic Thinking Domain: Calm in Complexity—Those with Strategic Thinking strengths thrive when others feel stuck. They bring clarity to complex situations by asking better questions, seeing patterns, and keeping long-term goals in view.

Influencing Domain: Composure in Conflict—People with Influencing strengths shine when tensions run high and the stakes are visible. These individuals often step in when others hesitate.

The 34 CliftonStrengths themes are all leadership strengths because each one can help someone succeed, both as an individual and within a group. The 34 strengths are the qualities found in successful people. When asked why 34, Gallup says that, like the keys on a piano, they had to stop somewhere!

The premises of Gallup Strengths are these:

- Themes are neutral.

- Themes are not labels.
- Lead with positive intent.
- Differences are an advantage.
- People need one another … to multiply the excellence!

The 34 themes fall into four domains: Strategic Thinking, Relationship Building, Influencing, and Executing.

Strategic Thinking	Relationship Building	Influencing	Executing
• Analytical	• Adaptability	• Activator	• Achiever
• Context	• Connectedness	• Command	• Arranger
• Futuristic	• Developer	• Communication	• Belief
• Ideation	• Empathy	• Competition	• Consistency
• Input	• Harmony	• Maximizer	• Deliberative
• Intellection	• Includer	• Self-Assurance	• Discipline
• Learner	• Individualization	• Significance	• Focus
• Srategic	• Positivity	• Woo	• Responsibility
	• Relator		• Restorative

Employee engagement refers to the involvement and enthusiasm of employees in both their work and the workplace. Highly engaged teams outperform the rest in business outcomes that are critical to the success of your organization. In other words, employees greatly impact the customer experience and response. Customers feel the energy of a business through the employees and choose to continue supporting that company, or not, based on the experience.

I recently had two very different experiences at the same business on two sequential days. The first day, an employee provided the standard "have a good day" with no enthusiasm or sincerity in her voice. It sounded rote and depressing.

A different employee on the second day made the same comment with cheerfulness and sincerity. What a difference! Successful companies pay attention to the company environment and to each of their "internal" customers.

At the time of this writing, recent Gallup research showed a decline in employee engagement in their jobs and an increase in active disengagement. Jim Harter, Chief Scientist for Gallup's workplace management practice, provided the following summarized information:

In 2020, 36% of U.S. employees were engaged in their work. By January 2025, employee engagement had dropped to 31%. Only 18% of the workforce reported being extremely satisfied with their jobs, and 51% were watching for or actively seeking a new job.

Gallup research indicates that "each percentage point gain or drop in engagement represents approximately 1.6 million full- or part-time employees in the United States." The employee engagement trend is important for organizational leaders because declines signal a potential vulnerability for business.

Gallup noted that the engagement elements that declined the most from the pre-pandemic record-high engagement ratio in 2019 to 2022 were:

- clarity of expectations
- connection to the mission or purpose of the company
- opportunities to learn and grow
- opportunities to do what employees do best
- feeling cared about at work

Gallup also found a six-point decline in the percentage of employees who are extremely satisfied with their organization as a place to work.

These are all indications that employees are feeling more disconnected from their employers.[6]

Younger workers' engagement was impacted more than that of older workers. In comparison to older workers, younger workers experienced more decline in:

- feeling cared about
- having someone who encourages their development
- opportunities to learn and grow
- their opinions counting
- having a best friend at work

Women experienced more decline in engagement than men did. In comparison to men, women saw larger declines in:

- feeling cared about at work
- having someone who encourages their development
- having progress discussions

For those in hybrid and fully on-site work locations, employee engagement declined from 2019 to 2022. Regardless of work location (including fully remote employees), organizational satisfaction, clarity of expectations, opportunities to do what you do best, and feeling connected to the organization's mission or purpose declined substantially.

The largest decline in employee engagement was among those in remote-ready jobs who are currently working fully on-site. It's worth noting that exclusively remote employees saw an increase of four points in "quiet quitting" (aka not engaged in their work and workplace).

---

[6] Inc. Gallup, "Indicator: Employee Engagement," Gallup.com, July 7, 2022, https://www.gallup.com/394373/indicator-employee-engagement.aspx.

Know thyself! Gallup research shows that individuals who use their strengths in their roles are more likely to be engaged in their jobs, report having an excellent quality of life, and strongly agree that they have the opportunity to do what they do best every day. In short, *the most effective leaders are always investing in their own strengths, while also investing in the strengths of their staff members.*

Gallup has spent decades answering the question, "How can we become better leaders?" In the largest study of its kind, by surveying over 14 million employees across 2,000 organizations, 559 job studies, and 360 general job demands, Gallup's scientific research identified the most essential competencies leaders need to achieve excellence. Whether those surveyed were CEOs, team leaders, or entrepreneurs, Gallup's research uncovered these seven universal behaviors that directly affect performance and outcomes:

1. **Build genuine connections.** Create partnerships, build trusting relationships with peers, followers, and networks, share ideas, and accomplish work.

2. **Develop people.** Prioritize ongoing development for every individual in the organization by investing in direct reports and creating a development culture where managers are trained to be coaches. Help others become more effective through strengths, expectations, and coaching.

3. **Lead change.** Model desired behaviors and challenge people to take responsibility for change by displaying the commitment you want followers to emulate and by providing a supportive environment that encourages people to develop great ideas and new efficiencies that align with goals and a stated vision.

4. **Inspire others.** Show people why their contributions matter. Energize them with a deep sense of meaning that reflects your greater mission, vision for the future, and the purpose-driven

promises you make to the people you serve. Encourage others through positivity, vision, confidence, challenges, and recognition.

5. **Think critically.** Take steps to sharpen your personal attentiveness, self-awareness, and coaching/development by getting the tools and support needed. Gather and evaluate information that leads to smart decisions.

6. **Communicate clearly.** Ask questions, listen actively, and fuel a culture with streamlined information sharing and informed decision-making. Share information regularly and concisely—up and down.

7. **Create accountability.** Hold yourself and your team responsible for performance. Define what employees are accountable for by setting and cascading goals and by infusing accountability in employee development. Accountability means engagement and taking ownership for the work, whether as a manager or an employee.[7]

Gallup encourages us to think about what "success" means for each of the seven skills, considering the disrupted and regularly interrupted workplace.

A key component for a highly functional organization is psychological safety, which creates a climate where people feel comfortable being themselves and expressing themselves freely. Each voice is heard and valued, and ideas are shared. "No one has a corner on all the good ideas."

Cultivating psychological safety allows staff members to feel a sense of ownership for the results and paves the way for increased engagement,

---

[7] Inc. Gallup, "Effective Leadership: What Makes a Good Leader: Gallup," Gallup.com, November 2, 2021, https://www.gallup.com/cliftonstrengths/en/356072/how-to-be-better-leader.aspx#ite-356345.

continuous improvement, and stronger collaboration. Staff members are allowed to bring their authentic selves to work in a productive way, which in turn influences business outcomes in positive and measurable ways.

Strategies to Create a Psychologically Safe Workplace[8] (from Lori Stohs)

1. **Lead with Vulnerability**
   - Show that it's okay not to have all the answers.
   - Share personal experiences of learning from failure to create an environment where people feel safe to learn and contribute.
   - Encourage leaders to model openness and authenticity.

2. **Encourage Open Dialogue & Communication**
   - Invite diverse perspectives and reinforce every voice, no matter the role or experience level.
   - Normalize asking questions and seeking clarification.
   - Set expectations that all ideas and concerns are welcome.
   - Promote active listening.
   - Address conflicts constructively, reinforcing that differences in opinion drive better results.

3. **Create a Culture of Learning**
   - Shift the mindset from failure to growth by focusing on lessons learned.
   - Provide consistent, timely feedback that is constructive and supportive.

---

[8] "Psychological Safety," Marketing, Automation & Email Platform, accessed August 26, 2025, https://mailchi.mp/loristohs.com/psychological-safety.

○ Celebrate experimentation and innovation, even when the outcome isn't perfect.

4. **Recognize and Reinforce Positive Behaviors**

○ Publicly acknowledge contributions and ideas.

○ Reward risk-taking and initiative, not just successful outcomes.

○ Encourage peer recognition to foster a supportive team dynamic.

From Gallup, we must focus on what we are already good at doing, lean into our natural abilities, and use them to grow in areas where we struggle.

Counter doubt with development; upskill yourself through the seven Gallup competencies. Focus on improving one skill each quarter; continue building by adding a new one each following quarter until all are solid skills.

As experience has taught me, psychological safety is not a "one and done" either. Aim for continuous process improvement in all areas! Great leaders know that development is a necessity—not a "nice to have." They're obsessed with personal growth and relentlessly focused on growing their leadership abilities. Strong leaders start with the "man or woman in the mirror."

CHAPTER FIVE

ON BEING A LEADER

What first comes to your mind when you hear the word "leader"? What does "leader" mean to you? Is it Chief, Director, Administrator, Manager, Ruler, Commander, Head, Officer, Boss, Executive, President, Guide, Luminary, Pioneer, or Pacesetter? What?

Unfortunately, the dictionary definition offers little help. A leader is "a person or thing that leads" or "a guiding or directing head (as of an army, movement, political group, music group)."

Gallup's comment on Boss's Day 2023 was as follows:

> "Today isn't your average Boss's Day. Yes, we're honoring bosses, managers, and leaders everywhere, but we're adding a twist: We want to especially celebrate the managers who have dropped the traditional command-and-control style—which doesn't work with today's workforce—and have instead **chosen to coach their employees**."

Managers influence team engagement and performance more than any other factor in your organization. That's not an exaggeration: **70% of the variance in team engagement** is determined solely by the manager. Gallup has been studying engagement, dividing the working population into three general categories:

- Engaged
- Not engaged
- Actively disengaged

Well-being and "quiet quitting" have become hot-button terms and seem to be directly related. Gallup's definition of not engaged means the staff member is *psychologically unattached to the work and company, and the individual puts in time but neither energy nor passion into his or her work.*

Considering the following statistics from Gallup in January 2025, even *before* the upheaval from current federal administrative tactics, employers have much work to do.

Gallup research comparing employees who are **engaged but not thriving in life** with those who are **engaged and thriving (have well-being)** found that those in the former group report the following risks:

- 61% higher likelihood of burnout often or always
- 48% higher likelihood of daily stress
- 66% higher likelihood of daily worry
- 2X the rate of daily sadness and anger[9]

Well-being includes all the things that are important to each of us, what we think about, and how we experience our lives.

The foundational aspects of well-being are:

- **Career**—You like what you do every day.
- **Social**—You have meaningful friendships in your life.

[9] Ryan Pendell, "U.S. Employee Life Evaluation Hits New Record Low," Gallup.com, April 23, 2025, https://www.gallup.com/workplace/653396/employee-life-evaluation-hits-new-record-low.aspx?utm_source=gallup_brand&utm_medium=email&utm_campaign=gallup_at_work_november_11192025&utm_term=information&utm_content=image_imagelink_1.

- **Financial**—You manage your money well.
- **Physical**—You have energy to get things done.
- **Community**—You like where you live.

Work hours consume a huge portion of our lives. I would prefer "life-work balance" to "work-life balance," but the reality is that many, if not most, of us spend more waking hours at work than we do with our families! **"Career well-being is the foundation of the *best possible life*, and your job and your manager are the two strongest links to a thriving life."** That's rather depressing when the manager has the same needs and falls into the category of those who too often don't get the support needed for engagement and well-being. That said, is it any wonder that growing leaders appear to be a challenge?

In a 2024 Gallup at a Work Summit session on succession planning titled *Enhancing Leadership Team Effectiveness Through Strengths*, the following statistics were provided by Vibhas Ratanjee.

Is Leadership Still Cool?

34% never want to become managers.

39% don't want to be promoted.

51% are content with no advancement opportunities, if they're in a role they like.

43-49% Gen Z don't feel what they do each day is interesting, important or motivating.

7-Point decline in the percentage of engaged older millennials (from 39% to 32%).

Managers have the responsibility to both engage and hold accountable staff members reporting to them. *We must also keep in mind that managers at all levels need the same support, engagement, and accountability!*

Hybrid and remote work are likely here to stay, though recent decisions seem to have politicized the issue.

Employees who work a hybrid schedule actually feel more connected to the organizational culture. Unfortunately, managers feel less so. Lack of support for managers likely discourages those who can and have the ability to move up from ever wanting to do so.

I was recently told of a pretty high-level manager who flat out told her entire department that "she was not responsible for their morale"! This same administrator, in her very first meeting with the department, did not introduce herself and started the meeting by saying, "This will be the meeting of NO."

How do you think morale is going there, and how many good people will leave before someone figures out that being a leader requires more? Yes, we are each as happy as we make up our minds to be (Abraham Lincoln's words, not mine), but outside factors certainly influence our sense of well-being. In recent months, so many similar scenarios have been shared with me.

In a Gallup landmark study of 10,000 employees, the leadership skills at the top of the list of what matter most to employees and enable them to achieve their best are:

- **Trust**—the foundation of leadership
- **Compassion**—caring about "followers" as whole people
- **Stability**—calm, assured leaders feel reliable
- **Hope**—imagines a future that can be better than the present

My thoughts: Walking the walk is more effective than talking the talk.

- Trust is the very foundation of leadership, both in trusting your staff members to do their work and in staff members knowing that you, the leader, are honest and transparent. "What you see is what you get!" Trust is built and earned, not awarded by position.

- Seeing each staff member as an individual and discretely empathizing when challenges occur demonstrates compassion, but only if it is genuine. Staff members are not your "children," but I believe strong leaders care about staff like family. Years ago, Erma Bombeck wrote a column on her favorite child. The essence of her thoughtful exposé was that her favorite child was the one who needed her most at the time.

- Stability will never be felt if the "leader" is inconsistent—or acts/reacts from emotion instead of thoughtful logic. Some in this category seem to get so caught up in emotion that they often don't even remember the directions previously given to staff!

- Trust, compassion, and stability combined with a positive outlook and solid long-range planning lead to "Hope" for a better future. A high or frequent staff turnover rate is often indicative of the absence of one or more of these attributes.

So, do we have a leadership problem? The following are my own thoughts interspersed with common definitions.

1. **The Peter Principle: The principle that members of a hierarchy are promoted until they reach the level at which they are no longer competent.**[10]

   Too often, the assumption is that someone who is doing a great job in a current position must be ready for the next level. Unfortunately, that next level often requires a different skill set, which hasn't been considered and/or training hasn't been provided. Promotion without preparation then leads to failure—and great

[10] Laurence F. Peter and Raymond Hull, *The Peter Principle* (New York: William Morrow, 1969).

frustration for the one promoted and those newly supervised by that individual.

Another common fallacy is that it's all about the bottom line. Though that is important in business and even in nonprofit work, Gallup's research, shared later, says something very different.

2. **The Micromanager: Do as I say ... power and control**

One-question test to identify a micromanager: *Is the team customer-obsessed or boss-obsessed?* (The only thing that matters to a boss-obsessed team is what the boss thinks—not mission, not revenue, not customers.)

If your micromanaging supervisor says, "Do what you want!",

DO <u>NOT</u> DO WHAT YOU WANT!

Stand still! Do not blink! Don't even breathe!

DO <u>NOT</u> DO WHAT YOU WANT! Just play dead!

Let's face it! It is impossible to negotiate with someone who has power over you and insists on defeating you! I have yet to figure out whether it is fear, a prior bad experience, or something else that makes someone a micromanager.

In the article "The Ultimate Guide to Micromanagers: Signs, Causes, Solutions," Gallup authors Ben Wigert and Ryan Pendell provide signs of micromanagement in teams and organizations:

- Boss-obsessed rather than customer-obsessed
- Every decision must be approved by the manager who makes demands without having the full context about what's happening.
- Every conversation with the boss feels like a performance review; employees are afraid to share their opinions and do less-than-best work in order to pander to leadership.

- Constant project bottlenecks due to excessive meetings, gate-keeping, and stakeholders
- Lack of new leaders coming up through the ranks; turnover of talented experts; stifled creativity, innovation, and agility[11]

Micromanaged teams can have a *veneer* of happiness and positivity, but the outcomes mirror those of unhappy teams: fear, paralysis, and dishonesty on the inside; unhappy customers, lower-quality products, and less competitive offerings on the outside.

In other words, a micromanaged team (or organization) is a disaster waiting to happen. Staff members are unhappy, which very quickly translates to unhappy customers.

Dealing with a micromanager strips the staff member of context, ownership, job autonomy, and creativity. A micromanager says, "Do it my way." They tell staff members how to accomplish something exactly step by step (often after the fact) and require perfect conformity to the micromanager's process.

The micromanager doesn't give context on how and why things are done this way and doesn't want to hear about improving or innovating to achieve better outcomes. Moreover, when a staff member doesn't follow the rules, the manager sees it as a sign of disrespect. The focus is on failure, mistakes, and weaknesses, rather than spotting potential and seeking continuous improvement.

Micromanaging can be particularly infuriating when the manager does not share the expertise of the team that person leads. Employees feel like they've been hired to provide their expert opinion, only to find that their opinion doesn't count.

---

[11] 1. Ben Wigert and Ryan Pendell, "The Ultimate Guide to Micromanagers: Signs, Causes, Solutions," Gallup.com, May 14, 2025, https://www.gallup.com/workplace/315530/ultimate-guide-micromanagers-signs-causes-solutions.aspx.

	MICROMANAGER	COACH
Context	Keeps you in the dark on the reasons behind decisions, priorities, goals.	Wants you to ask questions; explains the "why" behind changes.
Ownership	Owns your work, you don't; hogs the praise.	Wants you to have control and take responsibility for the final product; sings your praises to others.
Autonomy	"Do it my way. Or else." Every decision must go through them.	"How would you do it? Let's find the process that fits your style best." Trusts you to make some decisions on your own.
Creativity	Your opinion doesn't count; take no risks. The goal is error avoidance. If you mess up, it will be reflected in your performance rating and pay.	Assumes that part of your job is to figure out how to do this a better way, which requires trying new things. The goal is exceptional performance.

GALLUP

Micromanaging vs. Coaching

Micromanaging creates a transactional relationship in which the manager fixates on minor mistakes and focuses on a person's weaknesses and work style.

Great coaching is an ongoing relationship of support and trust that emerges out of a rhythm of collaborative conversations, leading to teamwork and shared accountability.

A great Coach/Manager:

- Respects the opinions of team members.
- Empowers team members to ask questions, take responsibility for their work, do their work in a way that makes sense to them, and develop more efficient and effective ways for achieving the same goals.
- Has frequent, two-way conversations with team members that lead to shared accountability for performance expectations.

3. Advancement for the wrong reasons

Added to the categories of the Peter Principle and Micromanagers are those "leaders" who seek positions simply to receive higher pay or to control others, or who are promoted for showing dominance and control, not respect and collegiality.

Simultaneously, there are companies with impressive mission and vision statements whose actions show little or nothing of either. Mission and vision statements seem to be PR tools. These entities, often equity and for-profit companies, hire for and focus entirely on the bottom line, which I have seen way too frequently in recent years. A red flag in any organization is a sales or admissions team that has higher status or makes more income than staff members with responsibility for ensuring customer service, safety, satisfaction, and results! Caring *first* about your customers—both internal and external—leads to a positive bottom line.

Research shows that companies, organizations, and institutions are much more likely to be successful if they focus on internal and external customer satisfaction, and *not* just the bottom line. A Gallup report, "The Will of the Workplace ...," includes an employee five-statement survey that Gallup's scientific research shows is the best predictor of organizational success going forward. ***It is based not on financial outcomes but on making the world a better place over the long term.*** Responses are on a scale of 1–5, from strongly disagree to strongly agree. The following five statements are the best predictors of organizational success going forward:

1. *If I raised a concern about ethics and integrity, I am confident my employer would do what is right.*
2. *At work, I am treated with respect.*
3. *There is someone at work who encourages my development.*
4. *My organization cares about my overall well-being.*
5. *My organization makes a positive impact on people and the planet.*

This data contradicts using the bottom line as the primary factor in effective leadership. Gallup encourages all companies and organizations to include these five statements in their evaluations in any format they use.

Why do you suppose positive responses from employees in these five areas indicate organizational success?

Staff members are more dedicated to their jobs:

- If they trust their supervisors and companies
- If they feel they matter
- If they think their work makes a difference and positively impacts the lives of "customers"
- If they think they have an opportunity for advancement

Of course, the bottom line is a key component! But without dedicated staff working hard for the customer and the organization, the bottom line will always be in jeopardy. In January 2025, Gallup found that employee pride in the quality of their company's products or services is at an all-time low (28%).[12]

Why It Matters

How employees feel about their organization's products and services has eroded across industries since the pandemic.

The industries that have seen the biggest declines include government, technology, and the transportation/warehouse industry.

The decline of employee pride doesn't just affect productivity; it directly influences how organizations meet customer expectations, creating ripple effects on customer satisfaction.

---

[12] Andy Kemp, "Employee Detachment Threatens Customer Satisfaction," Gallup.com, March 25, 2025, https://www.gallup.com/workplace/655607/employee-detachment-threatens-customer-satisfaction.aspx?utm_source=gallup_brand&utm_medium=email&utm_campaign=gallup_at_work_january_2_01282025&utm_term=information&utm_content=employee_detachment_threatens_customer_satisfaction_textlink_3.

Employers can boost employee pride by reconnecting the employee-customer feedback loop. The most effective teams:

- regularly discuss how they can better serve customers
- use customer feedback to adjust the products and services they offer.

Employees who strongly agree that their team embraces both these practices are more than twice as likely as other employees to report improvements in the quality, availability, and affordability of their organization's products and services in the past year.

Being a Leader (my thoughts):

- Is an *earned* privilege, not an entitlement.
- Has tremendous responsibility.
- Means you should listen more than you talk.
- Should mean you do the right thing, have high integrity, and ethical behavior.
- Requires that you address the hard stuff, the "crap."
- Provides an opportunity to make something purposeful from existing "pain," whether yours or that of others.
- Is not limited to or by position or hierarchy.

Remember the seven competencies reinforced by Gallup research, with my thoughts in italics. Leaders must:

1. **Build genuine connections.** Create partnerships, build trusting relationships with peers, followers, and networks, share ideas, and accomplish work.

2. **Develop people.** Prioritize ongoing development for every individual in the organization by investing in direct reports and creating a development culture where managers are trained

to be coaches. Help others become more effective through strengths, expectations, and coaching.

We must always remember that "customers" are both internal and external. No company will be successful in building strong external customers without paying attention to the needs of internal customers— staff, both your reports and those in other departments, who should/ MUST coordinate and collaborate with your department for the benefit of other customers! Organizations must work with managers so that each one knows how to support and is supporting their own reports and subsequently other internal customers.

3. **Lead change.** Model desired behaviors and challenge people to take responsibility for change by displaying the commitment you want followers to emulate and by providing a supportive environment that encourages people to develop great ideas and new efficiencies that align with goals and a stated vision.

4. **Inspire others.** Show people why their contributions matter. Energize them with a deep sense of meaning that reflects your greater mission, vision for the future, and the purpose-driven promises you make to the people you serve. Encourage others through positivity, vision, confidence, challenges, and recognition.

"Do as I say, not as I do" will create nothing but distrust. No leader can/should ever ask managers or staff to do that which they are unwilling or unable to do themselves.

5. **Think critically.** Take steps to sharpen your personal attentiveness, self-awareness, and coaching/development by getting the tools and support needed. Gather and evaluate information that leads to smart decisions.

Some years ago, I worked for a college administrator who had a business background. In his discussions with a for-profit postsecondary institution, our administrator concluded that our financial aid operation would gain efficiencies—both in time and cost—if we were to contract with the for-profit institution to complete verification, awarding, and possibly registration—following the business model used by that institution.

Before any conversation with the financial aid department, a small group of administrators, including me, the Financial Aid Director, were flown some distance to meet with the other institution's administrators. I appreciated the interest in supporting our understaffed office, but I was not feeling good about the approach.

By this time, industry articles, which I accessed and read regularly, indicated red flags within the for-profit institution's operations. I felt we would be putting our institution at risk if we followed this path, but our administration continued to meet on the issue and seemed convinced this was the way to go. Finally, at the end of one such meeting, I laid down several news stories and adamantly said, "When you lie down with dogs, you get up with fleas."

In hindsight, that action could have cost me my job, but had my school gone this route, I would have quit anyway. I had followed the rules and regulations for too many years to suddenly put our operation and my reputation at risk.

The decision to speak up more forcefully must have been the right choice. The possible contract with the for-profit was never mentioned again. The for-profit ultimately closed due to regulatory violations and loss of accreditation and financial aid.

Hiring decisions are generally made because of the training and expertise that contracted individuals have in their areas of responsibility. We, as leaders, should have more knowledge than those who don't work in our arenas every day. Listen first, but at any level of leadership, we must do our own research and be willing to advocate—to speak up—to risk—for our departments and ourselves. I shudder thinking about the headlines if our financial aid department had become part of that story.

6. **Communicate clearly.** Ask questions, listen actively, and fuel a culture with streamlined information sharing and informed decision-making. Share information regularly and concisely—up and down.

The example in #5 could also fit here. Leaders at all levels must never let themselves think they have all the answers or are the smartest people in the room. Continuous self-improvement must apply from the top down. Listen first, but be willing to share when appropriate—and necessary. Address the issue without criticizing the individual or placing blame.

Have you ever watched Hallmark movies? Yeah, I know! The plot—and the outcome—are both obvious within the first 60 seconds! But what happens in every single movie ... other than the leads going outside in formal gowns with no coats when snow is everywhere?!

In every movie, miscommunication or no communication results in life-changing assumptions being made—every time! A break-up years ago, moving across the country, turning down or accepting a job—all because two people who supposedly care deeply for each other don't communicate!

Though I hope the subject is business-related and not about one's love life, the same things happen in an office. Lack of communication and poor communication cause hard feelings, bad decisions, and poor or no results. Communication is key to almost everything!

7. **Create accountability.** Hold yourself and your team responsible for performance. Define what employees are accountable for by setting and cascading goals and by infusing accountability in employee development. Accountability means engagement and taking ownership of the work, whether as a manager or an employee.

Think about what "success" means for each of the seven skills and aim for continuous process improvement!

How many times in your life have you been asked or have you asked someone else, "So, what do you do?" Per another Gallup suggestion, what if we changed the question to, "What do you love to do?"

In their book, *Soar with Your Strengths*, Don Clifton and Paula Nelson highlighted five questions that help managers and each of us reveal the strengths of those we lead, serve, and love. Learning what people love to do can help us help them enjoy their work and become fully engaged in that work. We call these the five clues to talent. As managers of people, why wouldn't we want to maximize the talents of each of our staff members—and our own?

1. **Yearnings**: "What do you know you can do well but haven't yet done?" or "If you had an entire week with no previous work commitments, what would you spend your time doing?"

2. **Satisfaction**: A coach might ask, "What types of activities do you finish and think, 'I can't wait to do that again?' or 'What are you doing (at work or at play) when you truly enjoy yourself?'"

3. **Rapid Learning**: A coach might ask about learning, "What have you done well that you didn't need to have explained?" or "What activities do you execute naturally, but struggle to break down into steps for others?"

4. **Glimpses of Excellence**: "What have other people told you you're great at doing?" or "In your previous experience, what were you known for doing well?"

   Fortunately, we are not alone on this planet, and neither are our strengths. Others may offer clues to our own talents in the ways they recognize us. Success is a compilation of moments, and it takes a trained eye to notice these moments in everyday life.

Listen to these "experts," be they coaches, teachers, or children. Help others weave a story from these observed moments.

5. **Total Performance Excellence**: "What are you doing when time seems to disappear?"

The Hungarian psychologist Mihaly Csikszentmihalyi calls it "Flow," and describes the optimal state of intrinsic motivation. Getting staff and others to talk about this does not take heavy training. Simply inquire about times when all the pieces fell together. Whether you're a manager, colleague, coach, parent, or passenger on a plane, every single interaction is an opportunity to help others excel. It all starts by changing the conversation.

The basics of leadership—once again:

- **Build Trust**, the foundation of leadership—can't flip a switch; must be built over time and through conversations and actions
- **Have Genuine Compassion**—caring about team members as whole people
- **Provide Stability**—calm, assured leaders feel reliable for their teams (No Chicken Little syndrome!)
- **Exude Hope**—teams can imagine and work toward a future that is better than the present

What are the root causes of micromanagement? Micromanaging occurs when there is no relationship of trust and support between a manager and an employee. Managers don't trust employees because, frankly, they don't know them very well.

And vice versa. You can't flip a switch and turn on trust—it must be nurtured over time through conversations and actions. Managers must show they care and must prove to their team that they have the team's back. Strong leaders must have knowledge but also show stability by trusting and expecting those with specific skill sets to manage their responsibilities and strengthen results. A mantra of continuous improvement and recognition provides hope for all.

The essence of leadership is to move from a comfortable command and control approach to the sometimes uncomfortable requirement to become an "empowerer," a coach, a facilitator, and an educator.

Transformational Leadership, according to Gallup, means:

- becoming a skilled listener
- communicating clearly
- seeing and understanding systems and interdependencies at play to lead and support change where and when needed
- inspiring confidence in the future by aspiring, conceiving, and creating the outcomes you want

Strong leaders always remember that:

- Energy follows energy.
- We are all part of the systems we are trying to transform.
- Leadership is a collective capacity.

Boss vs. Leader

I wish I could give proper recognition and credit to the author of the following, but I have been unable to determine who it is. This pretty much says it all!

- A boss only sees things in black and white, while a leader also sees the grey.
- A boss likes to tell, while a leader prefers to teach.
- A boss likes being on a pedestal, above the fray, while a leader likes to be among those they lead.

- A boss gets lost in the details, while a leader keeps the big picture in mind.

- A boss rules by fear, while a leader inspires with trust.

- A boss displays great hubris, while a leader shows quiet humility.

- A boss likes to talk, while a leader prefers to listen.

- A boss wants to dictate, while a leader would rather collaborate.

- A boss outlines the "what," while the leader also always explains the "why."

- A boss thinks first about profit, while a leader thinks first about people.

- A boss gets lost in the process, while a leader gets absorbed in performance.

- A boss is a disabler, while a leader is an enabler.

- A boss criticizes, while a leader coaches.

- A boss manages to an end, while a leader serves for a purpose.

- A boss demotivates with impassiveness, while a leader inspires with caring and empathy.

I would also encourage all employees, and especially those in leadership positions, to read and absorb *QBQ!—The Question Behind the Question* by John G. Miller. Originally published in 2001 and updated and republished in 2016, *QBQ!* provides a practical approach for putting personal accountability into daily action to eliminate finger-pointing, blaming, procrastination, complaining, and victim thinking. The model will provide wonderful opportunities for discussion, mindset change, and personal/team effectiveness.

CHAPTER SIX

LET ME DO IT NOW

*"I expect to pass through this world but once; any good thing therefore that
I can do, or any kindness that I can show to any fellow creature, let me do
it now; let me not defer nor neglect it, for I shall not pass this way again."*

–Stephen Grellet,
French Quaker and missionary (1773–1855)

This quote from Stephen Grellet was framed and hung on my bedroom wall for many years. The words had also been set to music, an
anthem our high school church choir sang more than once when I was
directing.

Periodically, the melody floats into my memory and plays over and over
throughout the day, still speaking to me. "I will pass this way but once.
If there be any good that I can do, let me do it now … for I'll never
pass this way again."

Key Experiences

"Service presupposes the will first—and then experience."

–M.K. Gandhi

Not infrequently, the label "born leader" surfaces to describe an individual. Can that be true? I think not. Per decades of Gallup research, each of us is born with dominant talents, but those talents require knowledge and skill before any one of them becomes a strength that enhances leadership skills.

In addition to using your strengths and developing the seven competencies (universal behaviors), leadership development requires "opportunities to learn and grow." Identifying your own key experiences, both those that have brought you to where you are today and the ones you want to have, is critical for your development and can help you assist those you lead. Consider your past and present experiences and decide what you want for your future.

Key experiences are among the most critical components of leader success. Put simply, key experiences are events in a leader's life that result in learning, growth and/or increased capacity to effectively lead. Every role in every industry looks different, but the skills required to lead are largely the same, and key experiences are one of the foundational elements to leadership development anywhere.

Until I received a very recent article on leadership development from Gallup, I had seen no mention of "key experiences." For me, that component has had the most incredible impact on my life. If I were to share all of them, this book could get really long!

In no way should you leap to the conclusion that you need similar experiences to become a leader. Think about what you have already done and add where you can those opportunities that will help you grow.

A little background information: When my father was still a very young man, his parents and two sisters migrated from northern Missouri/ southern Iowa to California for better opportunities. Dad went with them for a while. These were the Depression years.

I'm unsure of the sequence, but I know he worked at a packing plant and a gas station at different times before completing his college degrees in multiple states. I grew up hesitant to drink Coca-Cola because Dad told us they used it to clean the gas pumps! Decades ago, it must have been pretty acidic.

By the time Dad quit taking college classes, he had enough hours for his doctorate, but he completed the work to become a school superintendent before his formal education was complete.

Because Dad's family was all in California, we kids were loaded in the car about every three to four years for a road trip from Iowa to California. Driving through the desert without air conditioning—sometimes at night—made for "memories." I can still mentally picture cars and trucks with canvas bags of water tied to the front of the vehicles to cool the radiators.

Our first few trips were also before President Eisenhower initiated the interstate system, primarily to assist the country's defense system following WWII. Trips were not coast-to-coast, traveling 75 miles per hour on divided highways! Route 66 was real, and "motels" were of the cabin variety. What I remember most is that Dad took different routes on each trip, with the purpose of seeing every National Park and point of interest between Iowa and California—Estes Park, the Great Salt Lake and Salt Lake City, Bryce Canyon, Zion, Grand Canyon, Petrified Forest, and the Painted Desert.

I wasn't very old when I saw my first Indian dance. I think it was at night at the Grand Canyon. Something so new and unusual was both beautiful and a bit frightening. The picture is still imprinted on my mind.

Once in California, my aunt and uncle made sure we saw Marineland of the Pacific, Knotts Berry Farm, and later Disneyland and Universal Studios—and always the beach. While swimming at one of the Southern California beaches with my cousins as a young teenager, I experienced a rip current. The Coast Guard came by telling everyone to get to shore, but the current was already pulling me out.

Amazingly, I had watched a program a few short months before that instructed anyone caught in a rip current to swim parallel to the shore until out of the rip current and able to turn back to shore. Obviously, I survived, ever grateful for unexpected learning, which seemed interesting but rather useless at the time.

My aunt and uncle's home was not fancy, but a very nice and spacious ranch with an outdoor fireplace on the large, finished surface in the back and a large garage with a playroom and extra beds on the floor above.

The land around their home was in citrus groves, not yet "developed" and very peaceful. We picked oranges and lemons from their orchard and ate foods we rarely, if ever, got in Iowa. Boxes of citrus fruits from California were often Christmas presents for our family. One year while staying at Balboa, I had my first soft ice cream and first and only chocolate-covered frozen banana.

Dad's job as school superintendent was pretty "all-inclusive." My little brother and I drove with Dad one year to Arkansas to finalize arrangements for a new school bus. We arrived on Sugar Loaf Mountain after dark and pulled into a driveway that we thought was the correct one.

To our horror, men met us at the drive with guns pointed at us. Apparently, their heavy equipment had recently been sabotaged with sugar or sand in the gas tanks, causing no small amount of damage. When the men realized we were not the threat, they gave us directions, and we went on our way—unharmed, but definitely unnerved.

On other family trips, Dad took us to the Ozarks, and on one trip to Kentucky, Tennessee, and Mississippi, the only trip not to see family.

In Kentucky, we went to several racehorse farms, one being the home of Man o' War, where a beautiful statue sat above his grave. One of the horses had a goat as its mascot that followed the horse everywhere.

That trip, which wasn't long, had to be a splurge because we stayed at the first-ever Holiday Inn in Memphis one night. We four girls, basically the oldest four children, had our own room, connected to our parents' room, of course. We saw "Room Service" on a flyer and ordered ice water!

The image of an elderly black gentleman driving his horse and wagon down the highway is another picture and contrast forever imprinted on my mind. Recently, on one of my trips back and forth from Virginia to Iowa, I spent a day at the Kentucky Horse Park and again saw the incredible statue of Man o' War above his grave, where it has been moved. What an incredible animal! His stride was 28 feet, two and a half feet longer than that of Secretariat and four feet longer than that of John Henry, both storied champions—all leaders, memorialized at the Kentucky Horse Park.

I signed up for a horseback ride around the perimeter of the park. By the time the ride ended, my horse, which was supposedly a bit of a problem, followed me to the exit. I think he would have gladly gone home with me. Animals, too, can tell when they are loved.

On the trip when I was a child, I remember my dad ordering a chicken-fried steak for dinner one evening. Not being aware of the southern influence and extravagant use of pepper, the dish was almost too hot for Dad to eat. Dad suffered before wasting food—and drank a LOT of water! We also drove into Mississippi to visit a polled Hereford farm, which was apparently unusual at the time.

When our own children were growing up, we had many opportunities to travel both for pleasure and business conferences. On any occasion, we tried to see as much of the country as possible. Our first trip "with children" was when our firstborn was four months old! We drove from Nebraska through the Dakotas and as far north as Regina, Saskatchewan, home of the Royal Canadian Mounted Police, then down through eastern Montana and Wyoming, where we visited my aunt and uncle and enjoyed the hot springs at Thermopolis.

As we were driving north from Bismarck, we were stopped by multiple patrol cars and officers with guns pointed at us over the hoods of their cars! We were totally ignorant that a bank robbery had occurred, and the culprits were likely headed into Canada. No, we were not arrested! Enough with the guns, already!

The only additional danger on that trip was when I was opening a hotel door with a baby in my arms. A large insect was attempting to go under the door. I was trying to scrape it out from under the door with my sandals, until my husband, who had taught in Arizona, yelled, "What are you doing?! That is a scorpion!" I had no idea a scorpion could be that far north—or what a scorpion even looked like!

With two children under four and a babysitter, we drove to California in 1970 to visit my aunt and uncle. As we crossed the Arizona/California border near Yuma, a driver coming toward us fell asleep at the wheel, crossed the median, and totaled our car.

Fortunately, we had only nicks and bruises, unfortunately, some of which were on our 19-month-old daughter's back from my holding her so tightly. Cars didn't yet have seatbelts or require car seats for children. My uncle, having more resources than I even realized, sent a private plane over to pick us up so we wouldn't miss the dinner with cousins and their families that my aunt had planned for that evening.

As we were flying through the low mountain pass in California, the plane quit! The pilot quickly said, "It's okay. I was draining the tip tank and had to switch to the other tank." The engine quickly restarted, and we continued on our way—after I restarted my heart! Talk about a traumatic day!

My aunt and uncle had planned to be in Hawaii for several weeks and invited us to join them, which we did. They had rented a huge home on the northern shore of Oahu, where the kids had the beach totally to themselves daily. Touring Oahu included a boat ride to the USS Arizona Memorial. My mother lost a classmate who served on the USS Arizona at the time of the attack. Standing above the ship was an incredibly moving experience, to say the least.

During a stop to see the fabulous Kahala Hilton, we were in the lobby when who should walk down the staircase but Carol Burnett. I walked up to her with an outstretched hand and introduced myself. She greeted me warmly and unexpectedly waited for me to talk. I thought she would just keep walking and had not thought beyond "Hello." I couldn't think of another thing to say.

Carol Burnett: 90 Years of Laughter and Love aired recently, and I was laughing out loud at so many of her memorable skits and hilarious compatriots. Unlike many stars, her own characters were not heroes, and she never hesitated to make them laughable or the brunt of the humor. Still wish I could have thought of something noteworthy to say.

In early summer 2023, we attended the 100th anniversary of the high school building in Norfolk, Nebraska, where my husband served as principal after it became Norfolk Junior High. Johnny Carson graduated from that high school. We had a marvelous weekend visiting with friends and then attended the closing night of the Great American Comedy Festival, held annually at the new high school's Johnny Carson Theater. The headliner was Vicki Lawrence, a long-time member of Carol Burnett's cast as Mama. She was so inappropriate—and hilarious!

When our youngest was just two months old, we gained a new family member. My husband had volunteered our home temporarily while a new home was found for a German exchange student whose original placement was not good.

After a few weeks with us, Annette told my husband's sister that she would like to stay the rest of the year in our home. She was afraid to ask. What an amazing young woman!

To her credit and my amazement, she gave up living with a family that had a high school student in favor of the principal's family with three children under seven years of age—one a newborn! We didn't have an extra bedroom for her, and she shared a bed with our five-year-old daughter. Over 50 years later, we continue to stay in close communication and make more memories.

Annette returned to Iowa a few years after she graduated and traveled with us through the Black Hills, Custer Battlefield (which it was still called at the time), Glacier National Park, Banff, and Lake Louise, across British Columbia to Victoria Island and Seattle, and back through Salt Lake City. She was fascinated by Indian history, as am I.

Since that trip, Annette returned with her toddler son. Some years later, we met Annette and her husband in London. Another year, we met Annette and her son in Munich. Our granddaughter and I met Annette, her husband, and her now adult son in Paris, where our granddaughter celebrated her 21st birthday on our way to Uganda. Annette and her husband visited us in Iowa for Christmas, visited me in Virginia another year, and met me in NYC for several days on another trip.

Annette returned to Iowa for a visit in the spring of 2022 and the summer of 2024. Every year for over 50 years, we have talked at Christmas time. In December 2024, Annette came for my husband's funeral and shared personal thoughts at the service, as did each of our children. What a blessing she has been for all of us!

Annette recently sold her OB-GYN practice in Bremen, Germany, to a colleague but continues to assist her a few hours each week. Years ago, an elderly woman I met in a golf league told me, "Never pass up an opportunity to pee!" Traveling with Annette, our children, and grand-children, they heard that phrase frequently from me. Annette told me the saying is now all over Europe since she has said the same to each of her patients.

The unexpected addition of Annette to our family enriched all of our lives. I always called her our German "daughter," but she has gradually become more like a dear sister.

Our older daughter has had a somewhat similar, long-term friend-ship with a wonderful student, now a doctor, from Rwanda, whom she befriended in an airport because she was not afraid to reach out and care for someone who needed help at the moment. Our daugh-ter recently returned from Rwanda, where she not only attended her young friend's wedding but was asked to be the maid of honor.

Though I value education and think regular attendance is critical, I also believe there is much to be gained from travel and new experiences. Our kids made up schoolwork before we left, but we did take them out of school when conferences were held during school months.

As Mark Twain wrote, "Travel is fatal to prejudice, bigotry, and narrow-mindedness, and many of our people need it sorely on these accounts." He doesn't need my endorsement, but I couldn't agree more. I would be a professional traveler if I could only find someone to pay the bill!

On Mother's Day 2021, our older daughter posted the following, which had honestly not occurred to me and obviously made me cry:

> "… To my mom—a patient teacher, great creator of road trip games and sing-a-longs, and a beautiful example of how to reach out to, and lead, others. Mom taught us that the world

is much bigger than us and if we want to make a difference, we'd better get comfortable with being uncomfortable. She took us to Indian reservations, the State Penitentiary, every historical site we passed on our cross-country adventures, and introduced us to people from all walks of life—all of whom were welcome in our family ..."

Recently, our daughter reiterated, "We stopped at *every* single brown sign!" Keep in mind that there weren't quite as many then!

In more recent years, grandchildren have traveled with us or me on numerous occasions, including Nashville, Virginia Beach, Monticello, New York City, Tangier Island, Paris, and Uganda. As I write, a trip to the Four Corners is planned with our youngest daughter's three girls. We will visit Window Rock, Hubbell Trading Post, Canyon de Chelly, Mesa Verde, travel by steam train on the narrow-gauge railroad from Durango to Silverton and back, and spend time in Santa Fe.

I hope to continue these trips, which have created so many unforgettable memories, for as long as possible. Two grandchildren at different times spent a college semester with us in Virginia, which provided endless opportunities to see Virginia and the D.C. area.

After my youngest brother died of cancer in 2010, my sister-in-law has been my traveling companion on several major trips, including to Ireland and Scotland, the Atlantic Provinces, North and South Carolina and the Outer Banks, San Francisco, Yosemite and Napa Valley, and the northeast.

For all of these trips, I loved being the planner and booking our overnight stays and adventures. After our last sister-in-law trip, when I booked a beautiful A-frame cabin in the woods of upstate New York—with the bathroom 15-20 yards from the cabin—my sister-in-law might want to use a travel agent going forward! I swear the ad said nothing about that little inconvenience! Somehow, the lovely—and leaky—little camp toilet we had indoors did little to alleviate the discomfort, though laughter at the memory and at my expense has been healing.

Though 34 wonderful years of my adult life were spent as a Director of Financial Aid, I previously had a number of other work experiences that added greatly to my life. Other "paid" positions were as a French teacher, church choir director (adult and high school), handbell choir director, high school youth group director (and summer mission trip coordinator/sponsor for 10 such trips), book editor, and agent with Northwestern Mutual.

When our children were little, I chose to substitute teach so I could be home when needed. We were lucky to have older women who were willing to come into our home to care for the kids with little notice. They were like "bonus" grandmas for our children.

I substituted in chemistry, physics, home economics, and history—everything but French and Spanish, my major and minor. I remember teaching a unit on the Civil War to eighth graders in eastern Iowa while their teacher was out for two months with health concerns.

I learned far more teaching the subject than during my own studies of that era, which reinforced my understanding that teachers always learn the most, and later encouraged my visits to numerous Civil War battlefields when I lived in Virginia. As a colleague in Virginia so "eloquently" put it, "You can't spit in Virginia without hitting a Civil War battlefield."

Prior to moving to Nebraska and then Virginia, we lived in Iowa and Montana, where I was asked to direct adult and high school church choirs and handbell choirs. I had no "education" in music other than singing in the high school choir and small groups, playing saxophone in the concert, marching and dance bands, and taking piano lessons for a year or two until they got in the way of sports.

I had excellent instructors and loved music! My love of music was largely influenced by my biological mother's and father's families. Songs at my grandmother's piano included "It Is No Secret," "Mockingbird Hill," "You Are My Sunshine," and my introduction to "How Great Thou Art" shortly after it was published.

Without fail, family get-togethers ended with lengthy sing-alongs, usually of old favorites from past generations, which I dearly loved. My five uncles on my biological mom's side, whom I was told regularly closed up the bandstand on Saturday nights when they were younger, and my dad, all had beautiful voices. One uncle, an Irish tenor, previously sang with the USO. After retirement, my dad, who was also a tenor, sang with three dance bands and a men's chorus.

In one community, I was part of a women's music "club," though not nearly as educated in music as other members. I gave a program on WWII music and accompanied myself on an autoharp, or dulcimer. One of the songs was "The White Cliffs of Dover," which we sang at family sing-alongs, and is a hopeful message for today. Eighty years later, much of the world still longs for peace, freedom, love, and laughter.

Music has incredible power and influence. If one listens to the music of each decade or period of history, the music creates a roadmap of our lives. Music reflects the culture and events of each era, but also influences societal, cultural, and even political change.

On the lighter side, changing dance moves often leads to changes in dress, or vice versa, especially for women! The 1930s to the late 1940s were the Big Band era. Glenn Miller, who grew up 20 miles from my current home, volunteered for service in WWII and organized one of the first military bands to entertain the troops and keep morale high.

Though he was lost at sea on December 15, 1944, while crossing the English Channel for France, his iconic sound lives on today, as does the tradition of military bands and choirs. I didn't realize until recently that the Battle of the Bulge began on December 16, 1944. Pretty easy to make some assumptions at this point.

The '50s introduced rock 'n roll and *American Bandstand*. The Everly Brothers were from the town I now live in and greatly influenced groups like the Beatles. Believe it or not, when the Everly Brothers were young, they sang at the grand opening of the new grain elevator in my hometown!

The '60s included rock 'n roll, folk rock, jazz, rhythm and blues, and anti-war music. The '70s again reflected the times with disco, funk, every type of rock, soul, R&B, and jazz, and pushed back harder against the Vietnam War. Stations on iHeartRadio devote their entire genre to music from the '80s and '90s.

In many instances, determining whether culture and history influence music or music influences culture and history is challenging. It seems to be both. Music is available to the masses, and you don't have to sit down and read a book, social media, or an editorial to hear the message.

During my time with the high school church choir, I somehow initiated the purchase of four octaves of Schulmerich handbells. In addition to the high school choir, I then had the opportunity to start and direct four handbell choirs—two junior high, one high school, and an adult handbell choir.

I have no idea why handbells seemed like a good idea. I had no experience with them whatsoever, but I loved the sound and working with the different groups. I quickly realized that not everyone could or wished to sing, and that young men struggling with changing voices could still make beautiful music with handbells.

Somewhat out of the blue, I suggested to the senior pastor in the Presbyterian Church where I served that I start a summer mission trip for our high school choir members. The pastor fully supported the idea.

Students each contributed small amounts toward their trip costs three different times throughout the year as a commitment, a total of maybe $75, but we raised most of the money through labor auctions, creating and printing our own "Sing and Serve" salad and hors d'oeuvres cookbooks two different years, a taco stand at "Art in the Park," a Boar's Head Festival, and a musical.

The work and fun of being together, knowing we were earning the money for these trips, created fellowship and a close-knit team. With support from the students, I suggested that our choir be called "Roots and Wings." That title had been used for a 5K run at a Northwestern Mutual conference, indicating home office staff and agents in the field. Our choir used it to indicate that our roots were in Jesus Christ, and our wings would help us spread the word.

During our time at the Iowa church, before our family moved to Montana for my husband's work, we took trips to the Ozarks, the Crow Reservation in Montana, and coal country in Buckhorn, Kentucky.

We never used preplanned trips or vendors. After the first trip, I deliberately searched for destinations that would provide our conservative, midwestern teenagers the opportunity to learn about other cultures and people groups while assisting churches in low-income areas.

I determined a goal and direction and started making calls. The contacts were always so open to our proposals and were very willing for us to stay on site (after the first trip, when I didn't ask), saving overnight costs and providing a place for us to prepare our own meals. I don't recall ever hearing "No."

Worship services we provided always included choir music and hand-bell numbers, with the students doing as much of the service as possible. After the first two trips, we saw a need and provided Vacation Bible School (VBS) in Buckhorn, Kentucky. For trips following those from Iowa, we always provided VBS or served as camp counselors at each location, as those needs were significant.

My husband accompanied me on some trips. The father of two students and the mother of another also volunteered to travel with us as chaperones on several trips. Their input and assistance were invaluable, especially with the larger groups.

Parents, in general, were incredibly supportive of all our activities and travel. Had they not been supportive, none of this could have worked! Until recently, I had not thought about the level of trust parents had to have to allow their children to go on these adventures.

The Ozarks

Our initial trip was to test the plan, check costs, and get our feet wet! We provided worship for visitors and some staff in the little chapel at Silver Dollar City. We traveled to Eureka Springs, Arkansas, to see Christ of the Ozarks and the Passion Play.

We also enjoyed the interactive and historic "Shepherd of the Hills" outdoor pageant west of Branson. Instead of intermissions, the audience was called down to the football-field-size, outdoor "stage" to join a square dance and a second time to assist the bucket brigade in fighting a fire.

The pageant is based on Harold Bell Wright's 1907 book about life in the rugged Ozark Mountains of Missouri. From that perspective, this trip, too, was a cultural experience. "Shepherd of the Hills" is a wonderful production and is still going strong.

We went to one of the first "water slides," concrete runs that we rode down on mats. We also visited a fish hatchery (or as one of the girls kept saying, a "fich" hatchery), where we actually learned a lot about the life cycle of a fish. We laughed a lot! Our first choir trip was shorter, but the sense of accomplishment, fun, and fellowship whetted our appetites for more.

Crow Reservation

I have long had a deep interest in, awe of, and respect for Indian cultures, perhaps due to those very first experiences watching dancing when I was so young. As I was searching for our second destination, I remembered that my husband had a college friend who worked for the Bureau of Indian Affairs in Crow Agency, Montana. We contacted him and, through a Crow woman who worked with him, arranged the visit.

On the way to Montana, we went to Evans Plunge Hot Springs and spent the night in cabins in Custer State Park in the Black Hills. We almost ran into bison while walking to our cabins in the dark! We were fortunate to experience the Crazy Horse Memorial, where the daughter of Korczak Ziolkowski, the artist who created the memorial, gave us a personal tour. At that time, we could see all the outlines of the monument, but much detail remained to be completed.

I arranged for our high schoolers to provide a worship service under the faces of Mount Rushmore, which was attended by campers and visitors to the park. Another highlight of the area was experiencing "Jesus Christ, Super Star" at the Black Hills Playhouse. That performance actually prompted me to purchase "Tell It Like It Is," a Christian musical, which our high schoolers performed later in our church at home.

As part of our trip, we provided Sunday worship at the Crow Community Baptist Church and again at a second "white" Baptist Church that seemed to be a block or two away. My group of girls stayed in Lodge

Grass, in the home of Clara White Hip, the Crow woman who worked at the BIA.

Our stay was incredible. We enjoyed a boat ride and tour of Yellowtail Dam and Reservoir, and visited Little Bighorn Battlefield National Monument, which was still being called Custer Battlefield at the time. Our family had been there on our trip west with Annette.

Standing on the hills and walking across the battlefield created a spiritual experience that I will never forget. I could almost feel the battle and the souls of those who died there. The museum still contained Indian remains, and excavation and findings were ongoing across the land. Fortunately, all human remains have since been returned to the tribes for proper burial.

The Crow were actually scouts for Custer. They were at war with the Lakota Sioux and other tribes, whom they felt were trespassing on designated Crow land and raiding their camps and herds. I recently read Joseph Marshall III's book, *A Lakota History: The Journey of Crazy Horse*, which gives an interesting and contrasting Indian perspective of that era.

A Crow tribal member invited us to attend a pre-ceremony for a Sun Dance out on a hilltop away from town. It was very dark, with light coming only from a ceremonial fire, around which four men were chanting and smoking pipes. The smoke rose to the Great Spirit. What an honor to be invited to this amazing pre-ceremony!

At the time, I was unaware of the history. The Sun Dance had been banned by the U.S. Government through the Indian Act of 1895. In 1978, *the year right before our trip*, the American Indian Religious Freedom Act allowed the ceremony once again for contemporary tribes.

Timing is everything, but the invitation to attend such a sacred event was truly astonishing and filled with trust. We could have spent our time on the reservation and never known about the Sun Dance.

After the pre-ceremony, we were treated to a feast of four different berry puddings served out of the back of an old buckboard there on the hilltop. The moon was our only light. The night was an incredible experience that I never dreamed we would have and that will forever be a key experience in my life.

The last day before our departure, tribal members treated us to a feast of elk, buffalo, fry bread, and so much wonderful food. We headed back east, stopping to hike and admire Devil's Tower on the way, so blessed by the growth we had each experienced.

I have two major regrets. One of the Crow elders wanted to make me a pair of calf-high leather moccasins. Thinking I would be taking advantage of her, I said she didn't need to do that. In hindsight, I most likely offended her by declining her gift … a learning experience, to be sure.

The second regret is that I was invited to bring my family back for Crow Fair a little over a month later, and a teepee would be waiting for us. Crow Fair included a reenactment of the Battle of the Little Bighorn, Custer's Last Stand. Because the journey was not short and our children were fairly young, I didn't think that was possible. How I wish I had made it an absolute priority to get there!

In 1990, Clara White Hip Nomee, the woman with whom we stayed, became the first female chairperson of the Crow Tribe. She served five terms from 1990 to 2000.

At some point during her leadership, a television story told of the tribe searching for the remains of a lost chief. Miraculously, an elder's vision took them to a cave in Wyoming, where remains were found. With much ceremony, the remains were brought back to the Crow Reservation and interred there. I remember the newscast vividly, but have found nothing to confirm this story.

Clara's list of accomplishments as Chairwoman was extensive and impressive, but her tenure did not end well. Her contributions to the

Crow Nation and testimony from tribal officials and elders encouraged the judge to allow her to remain in office after she was convicted in 1998 of coercing appointees to allow her a land purchase from the tribe for well under market value, a felony theft of tribal land.

She fought off attempts to remove her from office but was then defeated in the 2000 election by Clifford Bird in Ground. Two years later, Bird in Ground was convicted of bribery by a federal court and sentenced to 37 months in prison.

What I have gathered through the years is that nepotism, distrust, and sometimes corruption make tribal leadership and life, in general, very challenging, as they often are in communities and countries where the traditional way of life has been destroyed and resources are scarce. Clara passed away on January 31, 2012.

Buckhorn, Kentucky

With the two previous trips going so well, our trip to Buckhorn in eastern Kentucky coal country was one of the largest. We chartered a bus and had 30 or more high schoolers, some even from other churches, who worked with us and sang in the choir all year in preparation for the trip.

When I think about high school church choir members getting up to sing *every* Sunday morning for an 8:00 a.m. worship service, it sounds a little like fiction! Amazingly, we always had good attendance. I know how fortunate I was to have a group of committed teenagers who loved what we had together. We started every service with our hand-bells ringing the Westminster Chimes, sang pretty impressive numbers, sometimes with handbells, and periodically included handbell numbers in the service.

During this time, I used my monthly stipend to buy a Yamaha studio piano. Because I couldn't find one that seemed to fit, I rather miraculously sat down at the piano and wrote an introit that our choir used regularly.

My piano skills were rudimentary, but I read music, knew the piano keyboard, and was able to put the introit on staff paper. I asked our organist if she would add accompaniment, and she graciously added chords, which she said were all that was needed. My composing was a one-and-done!

Our high school choir members knew our participation rules for the year and the trip rules and consequences of breaking them (an immediate trip home at their or their parents' expense). We hadn't been on the road to Kentucky for a whole day when some of the kids came to me to report that one of the senior girls had alcohol. The girl who brought it came from a large family with many adopted children and needed this trip more than just about anyone.

In a moment of wisdom, my rules became unimportant. I asked the group what they thought we should do. The consensus was that the alcohol would be poured out, and the girl would be allowed to continue on the trip. The decision was a sound one, and the issue never came up again.

At another point toward the end of the same trip, we were hiking in Mammoth Cave National Park. Some of our quite immature sophomore boys started hollering at some guys down in a valley, who then began running up the hill. No confrontation occurred, but a lesson was learned. The guys our rather mouthy and oblivious young men had antagonized were army men on R&R. Our young men were pretty quiet after that.

The Buckhorn Presbyterian Church, where we provided a week-long Vacation Bible School, was a beautiful log building with a cathedral ceiling in the sanctuary. A water line from frequent and recent floods was clearly visible at the point where the high walls met the rafters. Within a half-block up a slope from the church was an orphanage. The children came to VBS.

Our students were the teachers for VBS, leading the arts and crafts, singing, and everything else. Several years after we had moved from that community, I learned that one of the high school boys who had joined our choir and trip from another church had become a youth minister and had even written a children's book, *Guess Who Saves the Rain Forest?*, which I was given by a friend.

As a high schooler, this young man was quite an accomplished close-up magician. I remember the startled look on the face of one of the little boys in his class when Jeff "magically" seemed to pull the little boy's underpants out of his jeans. Of course, the little boy quickly realized that his clothing was intact.

On all of our trips, we visited cultural and historic sites along the way and in the area. Shopping malls and amusement parks were not the focus. On this trip to the heart of coal country, we went through the Kentucky Horse Park, Mammoth Cave, and experienced a Stephen Foster musical at My Old Kentucky Home State Park.

When our family moved to Montana, where my husband became District Agent for Northwestern Mutual later that same year, I left Storm Lake with such a heavy heart but with so many wonderful memories.

The high school choir gave us an amazing and emotional send-off party and a beautiful patchwork quilt with squares made by each choir member. I will cherish the quilt and memories forever. I just recently received very unexpected thank-you letters from two of the girls who participated in those trips decades ago. One shared the impact the trips had on her and her two closest friends, one of whom was the second to contact me. All three were wonderfully strong, young women. The first to write has since been a scout leader for a number of years—paying it forward—and recently returned to the west coast of the U.S. from living in New Zealand.

Life in Montana

In Montana, I became an agent for Northwestern Mutual and, through referrals, developed a wonderful clientele within the medical community. I also wrote our district agency newsletter, which I called "The Lagniappe," a Creole term meaning "a little something extra," often candy or a food gift, that merchants in Louisiana gave to their customers at the time of a purchase.

In addition to immediately falling in love with and frequenting Big Mountain Ski Resort, Flathead Lake, and Glacier National Park, I became the High School Youth Group Director at the Presbyterian Church. Our high schoolers met weekly, provided worship on occasion, and again started summer mission trips, which had not previously been done in that church.

On three trips while in Montana, we provided a week-long Vacation Bible School for a church on the Navajo Reservation in Arizona, served as camp leaders for an overnight youth camp in the mountains outside Taos, New Mexico, and were camp leaders for a day camp for children in Golden Gate Park, San Francisco.

Chinle and Nazlini, Arizona

My love and respect for native culture again guided me to the reservation, this time the Navajo Reservation in northeast Arizona and northwest New Mexico. Our son, the oldest of our three children, was finally old enough to go on this trip.

I contacted the pastor at the Presbyterian Church in Chinle, Arizona, and arranged for our group to stay in Chinle while providing Vacation Bible School 24 miles away, across the reservation, at the small church in Nazlini.

The church in Nazlini had no running water or indoor facilities. We saw men on horseback herding sheep along the way and traditional hogan homes. We met so many wonderful people and had children who came from miles away to attend VBS.

About the second or third day, as we were driving to Nazlini, we saw two little girls walking along the road whom we recognized as having been at

VBS. We stopped and asked if they wanted to ride, which they did. After VBS, we offered to take them home. We had driven back to the area where we picked them up and asked if their home was close. "A bit farther," they replied. We drove some distance to a fork in the road, and they pointed in the direction they lived. After driving several more miles, we finally reached their destination. They had walked many, MANY miles just to come to Vacation Bible School, as we learned many others had too. No one drove.

When we told the pastor at Chinle about the experience, he shared a story about Hoskie, the lay minister at Chinle. Hoskie was to lead communion at the church in Nazlini one Sunday morning that past winter. It had snowed about four inches, and with reservation vehicles and roads being what they were, Hoskie could not get his vehicle out of their driveway.

Hoskie and his wife bundled up their four children and walked the entire way to Nazlini so he could serve communion. I have thought about that so many times. In typical Caucasian communities, not only would most people not walk six blocks through the snow for church, let alone 20+ miles, but no one would have been at the church when they got there since the time for church had long passed!

On the reservation, the people saw Hoskie and his family coming and gathered. The exact hour was of no significance. "Indian time," a cultural understanding of time that prioritizes events and gatherings starting when everyone is ready rather than adhering strictly to a clock, has advantages!

Canyon de Chelly is right at Chinle. We were able to hike to the bottom, walk across the shallow river, and experience the ancient White House cliff dwellings at the bottom of the canyon. We were taken to a spire toward the end of the canyon known as Spider Woman Rock. Our host told us that legend had it that Spider Woman came down from the rock and took misbehaving children back to the top with her.

We visited Window Rock, the seat of government and the capital of the Navajo Nation. While we were on the reservation, but not at

Window Rock, Russell Means from the American Indian Movement (AIM) came to Window Rock. AIM was an activist group attempting to address the many inequities impacting tribal members across the country. At the time, AIM was treated as a radical movement, with a bit of fear and a lot of disrespect.

Another highlight of our trip was the Hubbell Trading Post, purchased by John Lorenzo Hubbell in 1878, 10 years after the Navajo were allowed to return to their homeland following their exile to Bosque Redondo, Fort Sumner, New Mexico. The trading post and family farm and buildings were sold to the National Park Service in 1967.

Almost everything owned by the Hubbell family in Ganado is part of the park. The trading post is still operated for the Park Service by a nonprofit, the Western National Parks Association. Whether reality or not, Hubbell is *credited* with the high quality of Navajo weaving and silversmithing as he demanded and promoted excellence in craftsmanship. Hmmm …

I recently read George Plimpton's *The Curious Case of Sidd Finch*, the fictitious, but somehow believable, story of an amazing baseball pitcher who was also training to be a Buddhist monk. (When I told my 11-year-old great-grandson, a phenom in his own right, about Sidd, he quickly told me that Sidd's pitching speed wasn't possible; Nolan Ryan held that record!)

Very briefly, toward the end of the book, the author tells of his father purchasing an Indian blanket in the Southwest and praising its perfect symmetry. The Indian man who sold it to him shook his head and told his father that the practice was always to weave a few mistakes into a blanket. Perfection meant arrogance, trying to match the gods. I recall being told that there was always one distinct thread that led off the edge of a weaving to let the spirit of the weaving out.

We rarely had health problems on these trips, but on this particular trip, one of our young women sprained her ankle, and a young man ran a pretty high temperature. We thought the young man might have contracted the virus that was spreading across the reservation. The virus was supposedly spread by rats, but I cannot confirm that.

Both incidents were very concerning and required stops for medical treatment. Though healing took time, our students recovered. Just as COVID had a tremendous impact among the Navajo, extended families living together, group gatherings, and inadequate health care meant more people becoming ill. Though I really don't ever want to know, I have thought many times about the possible difference in outcomes if our students and children didn't have good health insurance and access to excellent medical care.

The Grand Canyon, another stop along the way, is just west of the Navajo Reservation. Zion National Park and Bryce Canyon National Park are just north into Utah. We hit all three on several trips and even provided worship at the Grand Canyon on one such trip.

On another one of the trips on the way home from Arizona, I arranged for our group to see Bryce Canyon on horseback. The day was beautiful, and riding the rim of the canyon on horseback was peaceful and gorgeous—a memorable adventure.

When we dismounted after the ride, however, I nearly had a heart attack! The owner of the horse concession casually mentioned that we had such a large group that he had to break some new horses! I could have gone a lifetime without hearing that, though he apparently had trained them well. No one went over the edge!

Taos, New Mexico

The children with whom we worked at the weeklong overnight camp in the mountains, a few miles outside Taos, were Latinx, elementary-aged children. We served as counselors and instructors. My husband, Dee, traveled with us and helped with outdoor sports. I can still hear a little boy running toward him, hollering, "Mr. Dee! Mr. Dee! The ball went down to the reever!" Such fun … and the ball was retrieved!

Several local Latina ladies fixed meals for the campers and us. Needless to say, no one lost weight that week.

Taos is the site of numerous art museums and the multi-storied Taos Pueblo, which was constructed an estimated 1000 years ago. The buildings have thick walls made of clay mixed with grasses and straw, which help insulate against heat and cold. No running water or plumbing exists. Huge, beehive-shaped ovens called hornos sit next to dwellings and are used for baking. The ovens are heated with firewood, which makes managing the temperature a bit of an art or science.

Taos Pueblo is one of the oldest continuously inhabited communities in the country, if not the only one of that age. My older daughter and I recently revisited there. In addition to homes where some 30 people still live in 2025, Taos Pueblo houses several small shops where native arts and crafts are sold. Members of the tribe return to the Pueblo for worship and for special tribal events held throughout the year. Taos Pueblo is both a World Heritage Site and a National Historic Landmark.

Taos Pueblo, New Mexico

Side trips on different youth group trips included the Four Corners, where students could put hands and feet in four states at one time, and Mesa Verde National Park in southwest Colorado. We spent the night at the park and toured the magnificent ruins that housed hundreds of Pueblo people, the Anasazi or ancient ones, before they mysteriously moved away. We climbed log ladders and crawled through small openings to explore the ruins. I remember hearing in the museum about a recently unsealed jug of corn that was hundreds of years old. The corn sprouted, a seemingly unbelievable phenomenon.

In the same geographical area in northwest New Mexico is Chaco Culture National Historical Park and World Heritage Site, which was home to thousands of ancient Puebloan people between 850 and 1250 AD. Though I have tried to get there more than once, that has not happened as of this writing. Chaco Canyon is in a remote area in the middle of the Navajo Reservation in northwest New Mexico, with access roads that are not always passable by auto. Someday …

San Francisco, California

In a desire to work in inner-city San Francisco with additional unique cultures, I contacted the Japanese Presbyterian Church in "Japantown," an area not far from the better-known Chinatown.

We were immediately asked to work with their youth as camp counselors for a large day camp held in Golden Gate Park. Our older daughter was now old enough and was a counselor on this trip. Another incredible experience … this time almost three weeks long!

We stayed overnight in the church, which had security gates and barred windows all around. We never had any incidents, but there was a shooting right outside the church the very first night. The local high schoolers with whom we worked were of Japanese and Chinese descent, and the man who directed the park camp was a tall young man of Chinese descent.

Aparna Rajagopal wrote a wonderfully impactful article for the February 19, 2023, Sierra Club Newsletter. And I quote, "When I (Aparna) was asked to write about what it means to be AAPI in the environmental movement, I hesitated at first because I felt I couldn't really answer that question, at least not through just my own lens. The term 'Asian American Pacific Islander' (AAPI) flattens a group of people who hail from a whole hemisphere of our planet—a hemisphere with myriad histories, languages, foods, cultures, religions, and more—into a single four-letter acronym. It's a monochrome wash over communities that each have unique connections to land, water, wildlife, and being American."

Ms. Rajagopal included a series of biographical paragraphs that highlighted several women from different AAPI cultures, each of which demonstrates differences while sharing a common understanding of the world in which we live. My first thought jumped to an even larger people group that is considered "one" for many college forms and designations, AANAPI—Asian American, Native American, and Pacific Islander. An "SI" added on the end (AANAPISI) stands for "Serving Institutions."

Four decades ago, my own ignorance of Eastern cultures appeared on more than one occasion. On that San Francisco trip, I remember saying I loved oriental food, to which I heard, "What kind?" Hmmm … not too many options in Iowa or Montana at that time—each just termed "oriental"!

The primary argument at the church each evening among local high school camp counselors was what kind of rice we were having that evening for dinner—Japanese or Chinese? What??!! One was drier; the other was sticky … another learning experience.

One day, my young nephew, who was adopted by my sister and was half black, came in from Concord with cakes for our whole group. Lonnie is no longer living, and that day will always be a special memory for me.

His life—and death—have strengthened my determination to continuously work for racial justice and equity.

Our campers in Golden Gate Park numbered about 200 a day for the two weeks we were camp counselors, and they came from every country along the Pacific Rim. I remember one little girl, possibly from Indonesia, who spoke French and was quite the anomaly!

Each evening and on weekends, we experienced the sights of San Francisco. We visited a Buddhist Temple and walked all over Chinatown, the Presidio, Embarcadero, Fisherman's Wharf, and took the streetcar on several occasions. Ghirardelli Chocolates were still being made right there along the bay. We went to a revolving restaurant at the top of a hotel overlooking the bay and ate another time in "compartments" at a Chinese restaurant that, we learned, had originally been a brothel. I drove our 15-passenger van past the Painted Ladies (famous row houses in bright colors) and down Lombard Street, the so-called crookedest street in the world, which is not very long but extremely steep, with eight hairpin turns. It wasn't until we reached the bottom that I saw a sign that said, "No Vans Allowed"! Embarrassing ... but miraculously no ticket!

One weekend, we took a boat tour of the harbor, and on another occasion, boated to and toured Alcatraz Prison, which included the cell of the Birdman of Alcatraz. Alcatraz Prison closed in 1963, whether or not as a consequence of three men escaping from Alcatraz in 1962 and never being heard from again.

Another weekend, after we had provided Sunday morning worship for the church, the women of the church packed a lunch of jumbo shrimp and other treats (complete with chopsticks) for us to have a picnic, unlike any picnic we had ever experienced. I drove our group across the Golden Gate Bridge and through Muir Woods, had our delicious meal, then swam—and body surfed—in the chilly water at nearby Muir Beach. What a day for us all!

While we were at the church, the Japanese community was in the throes of the struggle for reparations after U.S. fear caused many Japanese on the West Coast to lose their properties and businesses and to be interred in camps during WWII.

Strangely, the building at my high school in Iowa, which was used for home economics, agriculture, and shop, had been moved in from Clarinda, Iowa, where it had been built in 1943 and used first as a German and then Japanese prisoner of war camp during WWII. Though not the same as the Japanese on the West Coast interred just because they were Japanese, the two were certainly related.

As we were driving out of San Francisco the last weekend, we were caught in a huge "traffic jam" of individuals participating in one of the first gay rights parades. Simultaneously, in almost the same area, supporters of the Ayatollah Khomeini were demonstrating. Needless to say, high school students and adults from northwest Montana had never experienced anything similar to these demonstrations. Sometimes, I feel like Forrest Gump. "Yeah, I was there."

I was recently back in San Francisco and walked several blocks from my boutique hotel to the Modern Art Museum, a wonderful facility. I was shocked to see so many homeless individuals. The city certainly had a different feel from our previous trip.

Montana State Penitentiary

Before leaving Montana, "divine intervention" led me to take our youth group to the Montana State Penitentiary in Deer Lodge to provide Sunday morning worship. As with so many of these life-changing decisions, I honestly don't know where that came from, but I contacted the prison chaplain and made the arrangements.

We heard hoots and hollers as we crossed the yard. I began visiting with a gentleman in the chapel, whom I thought was a guard. He was an inmate. Another conversation was with a man who had been incarcerated, released, and incarcerated a second time. I remember well his saying he couldn't wait to get back to prison. He never felt safer than here.

After the service, the Chaplain talked with our group. He asked if we had any idea who was in the service that morning. I clearly remember him saying, "Sixteen men convicted of first-degree murder were in worship with you."

I'm not sure what that true message was. Though we moved yet again before I could arrange a return visit to the Montana State Penitentiary, that original visit eventually led to a prison ministry at Nebraska State Penitentiary and development of an Alternatives to Violence Project program at the Omaha Correctional Center in Nebraska. "How do you find what fits? You don't. It finds you."

Life in Nebraska

We moved from Montana in late 1986 after my husband made the decision to return to school administration. He took an assistant principal's position in Nebraska in the fall of 1985. My brother told him about the opening, and we interviewed for the position on our way home to Montana after visiting family in Iowa. I say "we" interviewed because "we" did! That was the only interview for my husband that I was ever asked to attend.

I always say I left Montana kicking and screaming … I absolutely loved living there and accessing the beauty of the area. The General Agent in Montana would not allow us to take more than 10 clients each with us when we moved. In addition to my 10, I had several clients who wanted me to continue as their agent and signed a document requesting that I remain as their agent. I then returned annually for several years—a serious blessing—to service those accounts and visit friends.

As I was trying to rebuild my insurance business in Nebraska, I made a referred insurance call on the Dean of Students of a small college—and walked out as the Director of Financial Aid, the beginning of more than a 34-year career in Financial Aid. For real! Once again, how exactly did that happen?

After considering the possibility, I initially thought I could work part-time for the college and maintain my full-time insurance license. That worked for a few months until the college also wanted me to work in Admissions and help with international students. I then went full-time at the college and switched to a part-time insurance license, which I maintained for several more years.

When the Dean of Students asked me if I would take the job, I had to ask him, "What does a Director of Financial Aid do?" He still wanted me to take the job. In talking with him, he knew I understood finances, had worked a lot with students, and was active in church, and this was a small Bible college. In hindsight, he might have feared he would have to do financial aid himself!

One doesn't normally start as the Director, especially knowing nothing about financial aid. The Department of Education provided no training at that point in history. I spent the first week reading federal rules and regulations nonstop and then had the good fortune to attend our eight-state Rocky Mountain region's summer institute. At the end of that week, I literally thought my head would explode, but the support and encouragement of colleagues kept me in the profession.

At that time in history, computers were quite a new thing. I finally got a small Apple computer to use, but had to develop my own program for recording costs of attendance, financial need, and awards. Pell Grants were processed by bubbling individual paper forms for each student and mailing the sheets to the Department of Education. After a few years, technology was at the center of all things financial aid.

At this first college in Nebraska, I continued the push for mission trips and encouraged the Missions professor to start a summer mission program for prospective students, which I suggested we call "Cross Winds."

He and I sponsored separate trips where we created and taught Vacation Bible School for churches where resources were scarce. My trips with high school students, and usually one or two college students to assist, took me back to the Navajo Reservation and twice to the inner island of Jamaica. I took a group of students from another church back to Jamaica a third time after moving to a different college.

Red Sands, Arizona

Our first destination from Nebraska was to work with the Navajo Presbyterian Church in Winslow, Arizona, farther west than Chinle. Our younger daughter and my niece were travelers on this adventure.

Our group provided all the teaching and resources for a week-long Vacation Bible School for all age groups at Red Sands, literally out in the middle of the desert under a large tent miles from town. We were provided with a small travel trailer where we could store supplies and prepare crafts. I spent a bit too much time in that little oven and have had issues with heat stroke ever since.

VBS was in the evening due to the heat. We were to start at 6:00 and finish at 9:00. The first night, six o'clock came and went; we thought no one was going to come.

Patience has its rewards. At about 7:00, we had literally dozens of all ages arrive for VBS. After the first day, I put away my watch. We started when the crowd gathered and never quit until the generator ran out of gas sometime close to midnight! Indian time is real and has its benefits!

One evening, we arrived to find that our tent had been confiscated by a herd of steers looking for shade. As hard as we tried to "shoo" them out, they were having none of it. Apparently, steers don't "shoo." Eventually, one of the men got his horse and rope and drove them out so VBS could begin.

On this trip, we were privileged to be invited to Shungopavi, high up a steep road on Second Mesa of the Hopi Reservation. The Hopi Reservation sits on three high mesas in the middle of the Navajo Reservation in northeast Arizona. We climbed ladders to sit on top of houses to watch dancing in the plaza.

As I recall, this ceremony was for good crops. Hopi ceremonial dancers appear as kachinas—spirits of deities, natural elements, animals, or ancestors. The people travel some distance to gather evergreen boughs that are used in ceremonial dress. We saw eagles tied to rooftops and were told that native peoples are allowed by law to capture eaglets in the spring of the year. The eaglets are fed to maturity and then smothered in cornmeal in a spiritual ceremony, with body parts then used for ceremonial purposes as has been done for centuries.

While on Second Mesa, we visited potters and were able to purchase small pieces of Hopi pottery. We felt very honored to attend such a powerful ceremony and to be welcomed by the people of Second Mesa. The Hopi are considered northern "cousins" to the different Puebloan tribes.

Sunday morning worship was at the Navajo church at Red Sands. Children were allowed to quietly roam around and play, and were not forced to sit like little adults. I truly admired the decision and thought Caucasian churches could learn from that custom.

The service was mostly in Navajo and felt very spiritual, though we understood little of the language. We sang "Jesus Loves Me" in Navajo. Two of our prospective college students who served as teachers on this trip enrolled at the college in Nebraska, completed degrees in mission work, married each other, and spent years in the mission field.

Before leaving northeast Arizona, we were invited to a barbecue. The featured main course was goat, which was quite good but not a type of meat normally eaten by our group. The head of the goat was thrown into the fire, and the most respected tribal elder was given that delicacy.

We were honored by the presence of a State Senator, who was Navajo. His words have stayed with me all these years. "You come to the reservation, we work together and enjoy our time. Then you leave, and nothing has changed."

I was humbled, to say the least, and saddened by the reality of life on the reservation. Further attempts to understand and work with our indigenous brothers and sisters have included presentations at the National Indian Education Conference and at a Tribal College Conference in Montana.

I reached out to the Department of Education to volunteer my time working with the HBCUs and Tribal colleges and universities if they can find a niche for me, though the current climate in DC makes the possibility doubtful.

I'm still hopeful, but after reading *As Long as the Grass Shall Grow and Rivers Flow, A History of Native Americans* by Clifford E. Trafzer, and *Killers of the Flower Moon* by David Grann, I can't imagine why any Native American would trust a white person who wants to "help."

Jamaica

An alumnus of Nebraska Christian College was from Jamaica but lived in Kansas and had been returning to Jamaica annually to help churches in the mountains. The missions professor took a group to Jamaica, while I took the group to the Navajo Reservation.

The following year, I began working with our Kansas alumnus and made plans for a group of college students and prospective college students to provide VBS for churches in the inner island of Jamaica that would likely never be able to have a VBS.

On each of the three Jamaica trips that I organized, we worked with a handful of volunteers from other parts of the U.S. to develop and lead VBS in different churches up in the mountains.

Our youngest daughter, who was very blonde, was on two of those trips. The children had apparently not seen many, if any, blondes. Standing by her, touching her hair—and marriage proposals (14 in 10 days on one trip!)—were frequent occurrences. I realized pretty quickly that black children in totally Caucasian communities so often endured white children and adults touching their hair.

That first trip was intense ... and a blur! We provided VBS for three different churches at three different times in rural areas outside Waltham, a small village not too far from Mandeville.

The other two trips included one or two Vacation Bible Schools in remote areas. Like the Navajo Reservation, children walked for miles to come to VBS, especially on the trip when we were way up in the mountains in a very rural area with no public transportation of any sort.

We stayed in the home of Brother and Sister Banton in Waltham on each trip. Their young grandson, Rickie, and houseboy, Moses, were our constant companions. Brother Banton was the pastor at the church next to their house, but he had a masonry construction business with long work hours because the church was in a very poor area and was never able to support him and his family.

Sister Banton was a seamstress and had a booth in an open market at Christiana, a small town farther up in the mountains. She asked us to visit her one day, and we did so. When far from the coast, we saw no other Caucasians and were in very low-income areas. A group of young men met us as we arrived at the market, aiming very vulgar statements at us by saying things to Rickie and Moses. The boys were extremely embarrassed. We walked past the group and into the market to see Sister Banton.

When the group of young men learned that we were there to see Sister Banton, the leaders came to us with hands outstretched, saying, "Respect! Respect!" Unlike their original feelings toward us, they held Sister Banton in high regard and didn't want to offend her.

On another trip, Sister Banton traveled by bus to Kingston to buy material. When I asked her how her trip went, she said she spent the day running. I thought she was speaking figuratively until she told me she ran from shop to shop to avoid gunfire.

Whether or not it was this year, in July 1991, Nelson Mandela came to Kingston following his release from prison. The people were so anxious to see him that they mobbed the airport and filled the streets. At one point, the police began shooting in an attempt to protect Mandela, and four people were killed.

On each Jamaica trip, we slept on the floor at the Bantons' home and always worshiped with Brother Banton's congregation—sometimes for two or more hours at a time! The family was so gracious and welcoming. I always thought Sister Banton looked like and reminded me of my Swedish grandmother, whom I loved dearly, especially in her demeanor. She had such a warm and genuine smile.

On one of the trips, I heard a lot of racket in the attic. When I asked the boys about it, they said it was bats. I casually mentioned the bats to Brother Banton, who quickly corrected the boys, saying that what we heard were rats. I don't think I slept as well after that, but they apparently didn't want to see us either!

Each of our three trips to Jamaica was a travel adventure and a learning experience. Each time, we landed in Montego Bay, generally resting a day before heading into the mountains in the rental van.

After the Vacation Bible Schools, we usually took three to four days to relax and see the sights before flying back to the States. We took public transportation several times along the coast. The public buses carried more people than there were seats and hauled chickens, goats, vegetables, and all manner of goods.

On one trip, I secured the driver of a 15-passenger van to take us to Dunn's River Falls, thinking the van would just carry our group. When I could not move my head to count, I whispered for my daughter to count how many people were in the van—30! The door wouldn't shut, so some latecomers just hung onto the outside.

Side trips included Negril, Dunn's River Falls, Puerto Bueno (now called Discovery Bay), the site of Christopher Columbus's landing, and, of course, the beach at Montego Bay. We ate fiery jerk chicken and so much fresh fruit! My daughter reminded me about gnips, otherwise known as Spanish limes. The small, round fruit has a giant seed inside with just a thin layer of sweet fruit around it that has to be sucked off to be enjoyed. Peers (avocados) and bananas fresh off the tree, and hardo bread, a heavy, delicious bread we ate at every opportunity, are among our memories.

In Montego Bay, we stayed at a local hotel that was clean but very modest. Seeing the affluence of the huge hotels with walls all around and hovels right outside where the local residents lived was heartbreaking. It seemed that most of the money from the hotels left the country.

CHAPTER SEVEN

CONSIDER THE POSSIBILITIES

"Unless someone like you cares a whole awful lot, nothing is going to get better. It's not."

—The Lorax (by Dr. Seuss)

A dear friend and PEO sister has the above quote from *The Lorax* as a "footer" on her email. Seems like a perfect quote for a section on volunteer work, though it applies to all of life. Many of the opportunities I have had were really "volunteer work" or opportunities loosely related to employment.

Prison Ministry

The student body at the first college where I worked as the Director of Financial Aid was broken into small groups, called Care Groups, that each included males and females from all grade levels who met regularly for fellowship and service.

The concept was beneficial on so many levels, not the least of which was instant connections for students who sometimes struggle to feel part of a new environment. I was not a member of the denomination that supported the college, but I was somehow the only woman at that conservative school who was allowed to lead a Care Group of students. When men reached puberty, they were no longer to be taught by women.

After my experience in Montana, I suggested to our Care Group that we start a prison ministry at Nebraska State Penitentiary (NSP), a maximum-security men's prison in Lincoln. I contacted the prison and was put in touch with the prison chaplain. We worked closely with him and traveled to Lincoln several times each year to provide Sunday worship, which was greatly welcomed by inmates and staff alike, and provided our ministry majors and music majors with experiential learning and opportunities to lead.

Whether for the "right" reasons or not, the chaplain told me that we always had significantly greater numbers attending services when we were there. When I was hired at the neighboring four-year public college, I continued for some months to take a group of students to NSP for Sunday worship.

National Defense Language Institute

After moving to the public four-year college, I was invited, along with a few other financial aid directors across the country, to visit the National Defense Language Institute (NDLI) in Monterey, California.

As a foreign language major myself, I was especially interested and was very impressed with the immersion program, which has been so successful in training individuals to learn strategic languages.

We stayed in a lovely, small motel close to the wharf and were able to walk everywhere. The hotel didn't seem luxurious but was certainly exceptional. My room had a huge fireplace, a first for me, and the hotel hosted a happy hour each evening.

After the formal NDLI program, I took the historic adobe walking tour of the original government buildings in California. In the building that I believe was the original capital building, documents were under glass but accessible to peruse. I was impacted by wording in the original agreements, which said, "All documents would be written in both English and Spanish." My guess is that those pushing for English only at the time—and still—have no idea what the original laws said.

If everyone had the opportunity to access the National Defense Language Institute, learning a second language might be more easily accomplished. Having two additional languages in my high school and college curriculum—without the opportunity to "live" either language—demonstrated clearly for me how difficult attaining fluency in another language can be, especially English with all of our idiomatic expressions. I agree that having a common language is valuable, but we need to have a little grace for those who are desperately trying to learn English, especially as adults.

Alternatives to Violence Project (AVP)

After moving to the public four-year college as Director of Financial Aid, I recruited a colleague from the new school, and we continued the prison ministry. In May of 1997, while I was at the four-year public school, I was asked by a Catholic sister from Omaha to help start an Alternatives to Violence Project (AVP) at Omaha Correctional Center.

We first participated in an AVP workshop at South Dakota State Penitentiary, a very old territorial prison with walls many feet thick and 15 feet underground. I am not Catholic, and I have no idea how Sister Marian got my name.

During the years that we provided three-day AVP workshops for inmates, Sister Marian and I became great friends, worked so well together, and trained others to assist. We also held Train the Trainer weekends for inmates who had completed basic and advanced workshops so they could become co-facilitators with us.

Those co-facilitator positions were highly sought, valued, and respected by other inmates, and gave those trainers additional leadership skills. Prison administrators noticed a marked difference in the prison environment and welcomed us back as often as we could come in.

Each three-day workshop included 25-30 men. No guards were allowed in the room except during count. I never once felt frightened or disrespected and somehow knew that if anyone started an altercation, the other guys would take him down.

I also remember the heartache I felt when a former student walked into one of the workshops ... in prison for possession and selling. I wonder how many states have released those convicted of crimes that are now no longer crimes in those states.

Prison administrators and inmates knew that we would not share what happened in the workshops and would not advocate for the men in parole hearings. On one occasion, I wish we could have. Fear and violence were so ingrained in this young man that he immediately pulled an imaginary gun and shot during a role play. A family member was, at the time, working for his parole. Two weeks after parole was granted, he was shot and killed by police in a drug deal gone bad.

My colleague from the four-year public college who joined the prison ministry also became a good friend and part of AVP. Anneliese was a single mother with two children, a son who was in the military and a teenage daughter.

A few years after we started working together, Anneliese had a stroke. The hospital kept her alive until her son could return from deployment to see her one last time. I visited her while several of her friends were there, telling stories and laughing about all the good times they had together. I had never experienced such an afternoon. Though Anneliese was in a coma and on life support, they somehow knew she could hear them … another unique and uplifting experience I will never forget.

Alternatives to Violence workshops are typically three-day experiential workshops that focus on team building, communication, and creative conflict resolution. The central concept is Transforming Power, the ability each of us has to change a negative or potentially violent outcome into a positive or nonviolent one.

The five precepts are: Respect for Self, Care for Others, Expect the Best, Think Before Reacting, and Ask for a Nonviolent Solution. And, I would add, Always Consider the Other's Viewpoint.

One of the first exercises in AVP is called the Adjective Name Game. Facilitators and participants alike choose an aspirational and uplifting adjective name that starts with the same letter as their first name and is then combined with their first name. Throughout the workshop, participants initiate all comments by stating their own adjective names first and then addressing others using their adjective names.

My adjective name is Jumpstart Joan, which came to me quickly and stuck. Adjective names help each person see himself or herself and others in a positive light, which is vitally important for each of us, but especially for individuals who have been seen as "less than" and/or burdens on society.

AVP grew out of the 1960s Quaker Project on Community Conflict (QPCC). Inmates at Green Haven Prison, a maximum-security facility for males in New York state, had heard of QPCC and were part of that very first AVP workshop in 1975, which facilitator and inmates alike felt would fill a real need for inmates.

Since that time, many inmates and outside facilitators have added activities for basic, advanced, and facilitator workshops, which are now international. AVP celebrated 50 years at the 2025 conference in New York State.

In 1998, I attended the International AVP Conference in Houston, Texas, over Labor Day weekend. (We could have chosen a better season! It rained—and then quit, but it was so humid I couldn't tell the difference!) The structure for AVP International was developed at this conference, but due to poor internet and other communication challenges, AVP International did not become a functional reality until 2008.

During one breakout session in Houston in 1998, I was in a small room of maybe 30 people with teams from then current troubled spots all over the world: Northern Ireland, Cuba, Serbia/Herzegovina, El Salvador—you get the picture. What I quickly realized was that any one of their stories could be picked up and placed in another of those locations. The trouble always seemed to be about power and control by those who called themselves "leaders." The greater good was nowhere to be found.

Though most AVP workshops are held in prisons, the precepts apply anywhere. I held one weekend workshop at the community college where I was working by then, and actually gained another facilitator, a woman who had worked in remote areas of Papua New Guinea, a place I have always wanted to go.

At my last community college in Virginia, I used numerous AVP exercises as a way to rebuild community and trust among staff members, and again in a leadership workshop prior to a state financial aid conference.

Aids Orphans Education Trust (AOET)

Through a financial aid colleague and friend with whom I had presented on the DREAM Act at the NASFAA (National Association of Student Financial Aid Administrators) Conference in Seattle, I became acquainted with the Aids Orphans Education Trust (AOET). Paul had retired, and he and his wife, Jean, were looking for a way to give back when they found AOET and spent a month in Uganda to determine if the founders were legitimate and doing all they said they were.

A few years later, my husband and I made the decision to travel to Uganda with Paul and Jean. As volunteers were completing plans for our first mission trip to work with AOET in Uganda, totally separate from my work with college students, we were each asked to complete a skills sheet so that our efforts in Uganda could be maximized.

As a bit of an afterthought, I wrote that I was a trained facilitator in the Alternatives to Violence Project (AVP). Leaders in Uganda immediately asked me to go to northern Uganda to provide AVP workshops where the Lord's Resistance Army (LRA) was actively terrorizing the villages. The LRA regularly raided the villages and took what they wanted. Little boys were kidnapped and turned into soldiers for the LRA, and little girls were taken as sex slaves. At that time, an estimated 1300 babies had been born from these young girls.

More on Uganda later, but on that first trip, I facilitated a workshop for the mayor, council members, and a small group of schoolteachers in Lira and a second workshop for orphaned children, one of the most difficult workshops I have ever facilitated. At that time, AIDS—and violence—were taking the lives of many parents.

First AVP Workshop for LIRA Community Leaders

After that first workshop, one of the young men who accompanied us to Lira quietly observed, "These concepts really apply anywhere, don't they?" Yes! Yes, they do! As an example, had I not kept "Expect the Best" at the forefront of my thoughts when I went into a contentious meeting with a college president (who was angry because he wanted to make a student eligible for Federal Work Study who wasn't), the results of the meeting might not have turned out as they did. After using many of the exercises with our financial aid staff in northern Virginia, several staff members posted "Expect the Best" on their computers.

In any scenario where conflict can occur and emotions are high, having conflict resolution skills is paramount. I left my AVP notebook with Joseph, the young man who made the astute observation.

Conflict Resolution Workshops

Though the AVP model using experiential exercises is excellent, one doesn't always have the luxury of time to complete a full weekend of valuable exercises. **Conflict Resolution** was one of two topics I had the privilege of presenting at each of the eight state conferences in our RMASFAA region several years ago. We were able to use brief AVP exercises, but the concepts presented were more classroom-style for the workshops and included the following:

Conflict is the expressed struggle between at least two interdependent parties who perceive incompatible goals, scarce rewards, and interference from the other party.

In a conflict, both or all parties:

- Must be aware of the problem
- View one party's gain as the other party's loss
- Might believe there isn't enough of something to go around
- Are usually dependent on one another in some way

Conflicts are magnified if or when prejudicial viewpoints exist. ***Know yourself … you carry baggage!*** We ALL do! We are socialized to be biased.

Personal Conflict Styles

Nonassertive Behavior: Inability to express one's thoughts or feelings due to lack of confidence or skill

Direct Aggression: Where the non-asserter underreacts, this individual overreacts

Indirect Aggression: Expression of hostility in an obscure way

Assertion: Expression of thoughts, needs, and feelings—clearly and directly—without judging or dictating to others

The following includes concepts from psychiatrist Thomas Anthony Harris's self-help book, *I'm Ok—You're Ok.*

Non–Assertive Behavior	Direct Aggression	Indirect Aggression	Assertion
I'm not okay; you're okay.	I'm okay; you're not okay.	I'm okay; you're not okay, but I'm going to let you think you are.	I'm okay; you're okay.

Conflict Resolution Styles

- **Win-Lose:** One party gets what he/she wants: the other party comes up short.
- **Lose-Lose:** Neither side is satisfied with the outcome.
- **Win-Win:** Finding a solution that satisfies the needs of every-one involved

If win–win is so obviously the most desirable approach, why is it so rarely used?

- Lack of awareness that winning doesn't require defeat
- Conflicts are emotional; people react combatively
- Difficult to negotiate with someone who insists on defeating you

Six-Point Problem-Solving

1. Define the problem in terms of both people's needs.
2. Restate the problem in such a way as to include both people's needs.
3. Brainstorm alternative solutions.
4. Evaluate these solutions.
5. Decide on the best solution acceptable to all.
6. Later, at an agreed-upon time, evaluate how/if the chosen solution is working.

Listen first, **but there are levels of listening:**

- Level 1: Downloading (taking in information)
- Level 2: Positional (preparing response—tend to force own view or quit participating)
- Level 3: Curiosity (encouraging more discussion by asking questions)
- Level 4: Co-Creation (learning from each other; result can be synergy, when the whole is greater than the sum of its parts)

When we truly listen, we risk being changed!

The Franklin Reality Model of Behavior Modification— Hyrum W. Smith, co-founder of Franklin-Covey[13]

"Teach (and learn) correct principles, and they will govern themselves."

–Hyrum W. Smith, Franklin-Covey

A. **Human needs are the engine that drives the train.**

    1. To Live

    2. To Love and Be Loved

    3. To Have Variety in Life

    4. To Feel Important

B. **We each have a Belief Window (our Personal Principles).**

C. **Our Belief Window influences our Behavior Patterns— our rules (if … then).**

D. **The results are supposed to fill needs.**

    ○ If the results of your behavior do not meet your needs, there is an incorrect principle in your belief window.

    ○ Results take time to measure.

    ○ Growth is the process of changing principles in your belief window.

Six Steps to Use the Model:

    1. Identify the behavior patterns.

    2. Identify possible principles driving the behavior.

    3. Predict future behavior based on those principles.

    4. Identify alternative principles.

    5. Predict future behavior based on the new principles.

---

[13] Hyrum W. Smith and George Lee Andrews, *The 10 Natural Laws of Successful Time and Life Management* (Los Angeles, CA: Time Warner AudioBooks, 1993).

6. Compare steps #3 and #5.

Reminders:

- We have been socially conditioned to be biased.
- To think one is immune may be the height of naivete or arrogance.
- We can grow and change if we are willing to confront and unlearn prejudicial conditioning.
- Unlearning our biases means acquiring accurate information and experiences.

Reality Model

- If your self-worth is dependent on anything external, you are in big trouble.
- When the results of your behavior meet your needs over time, you experience inner peace.
- The mind naturally seeks harmony when presented with two opposing principles.

Though differences are emphasized in conflicts, our basic needs are the same. We all want:

- To live
- To love and be loved
- To have variety in our lives
- To be recognized for who we are and for what we have accomplished in our lives—to feel important

Effective supervisors, managers, and leaders *must*:

- Value diversity
- Be willing to share power and empower others
- Develop others

- Work for change

"One's philosophy is not expressed in words. It is expressed in the choices one makes. This process never ends until we die. And the choices we make are ultimately our responsibility."

—Eleanor Roosevelt

"Everybody lives downstream. What I do matters."

—Robin Wall Kimmerer

"Raise your words, not your voice. It is rain that grows flowers, not thunder."

—Rumi

"If you change the way you look at things, the things you look at change."

—Dr. Wayne Dyer

"We don't see things as they are. We see things as we are."

—Anais Nin

"Yesterday I was clever, so I wanted to change the world. Today I am wise, so I am changing myself."

—Rumi

Habitat for Humanity

When I chaired the Mission Committee at the Congregational Church, we initiated Norfolk Area Habitat for Humanity (HFH) in June 1994. A retired pastor and his wife served on the committee and had worked with HFH in another community. My family history of remodeling and construction in addition to full-time careers made HFH seem very doable.

Our committee successfully gained the support of most churches in Norfolk, making this endeavor a success. Monthly meetings moved from one church to the next, and board members represented a cross-section of the community. Personal religious beliefs were set aside as we worked together to build homes for those in need. We literally went to court to save our first family when they were about to be deported for a rather trivial error on their immigration papers.

Each year for several years, we held a banquet to recognize volunteers and to raise funds to help build more houses. For our HFH banquet in June 1996, I invited Millard and Linda Fuller, founders of Habitat for Humanity, to speak—not really thinking they would be able to attend. They could and did! Millard spoke at the banquet, and they stayed overnight in our home. What an honor and opportunity to meet and learn from individuals who have literally impacted lives around the world—and were friends of and builders with Jimmy and Rosalyn Carter! At one point, when the organization was facing challenges in several areas, Millard commented, "We always have Nebraska!"

After serving six years as President, my dear friend and colleague, who had worked with me from the beginning, assumed the Presidency and later became Executive Director.

A few years into our development, the head of the construction department at Northeast Community College began participating. His classes assisted with the builds, which provided much-needed help for us and hands-on experience in construction, electrical, plumbing, and heating for students in those college programs.

Over 30 homes have been built in Norfolk, and our chapter helped Wayne, Nebraska, start a chapter, as well. As I write this, the international office has implemented requirements that are challenging, if not impossible, for smaller chapters. Norfolk had money to build, but was hamstrung by new and demanding HFH rules. The decision was recently made to leave HFH and become part of The Fuller Center for Housing, also started by Millard and Linda Fuller. The change allows the Norfolk chapter to again build without HFH's restrictive, labor-intensive, supplemental requirements that are nearly impossible for small chapters.

Orphan Grain Train and Mercy Meals

A benefactor in the shipping business and a Lutheran minister in Norfolk started an organization that was eventually named Orphan Grain Train (OGT). An offshoot of that is an organization now called Mercy Meals, which packs nutritious, dried meal packets that can be shipped to families in need all over the world.

Both divisions depend on volunteers to assist the very few staff members. When we were still in Norfolk, the organization was in its infancy and has now grown to include chapters all over the United States and shipments for organizations and churches around the world. Years ago, we were part of a retired teachers' group that began packing meals at least once a week, a tradition that is ongoing these many years later.

When we shared with OGT the needs of AOET after our first trip to Uganda, we began planning a shipment. We raised the money to ship a cargo container of donated hospital beds, medical equipment, school desks, and a ton of textbooks and library books to the clinic and school at AOET.

We were later told that the used equipment made the AOET clinic in Bugembe, a village outside Jinja in southern Uganda, better equipped than the local hospital. AOET has medical personnel on staff and frequently has doctors and other trained medical staff among the volunteers who travel to Uganda with Paul and Jean. Each trip always includes rural health clinics in multiple villages outside Bugembe, which are set up wherever space or a building allows.

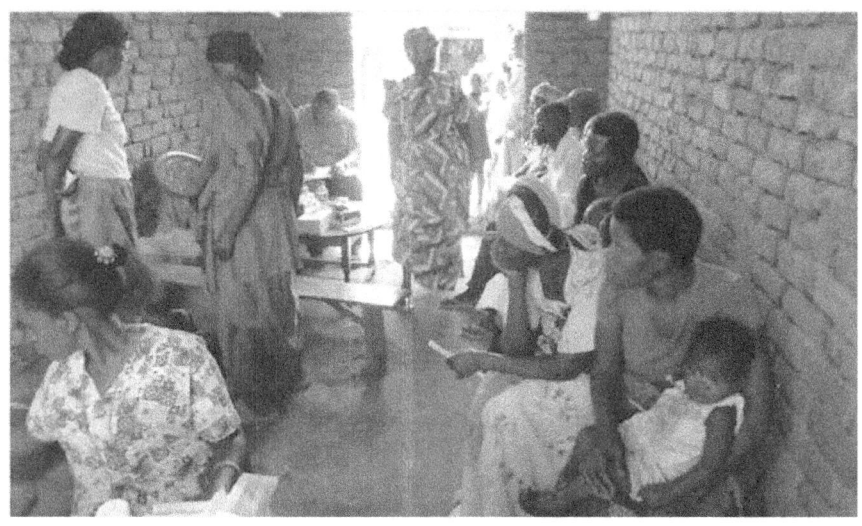

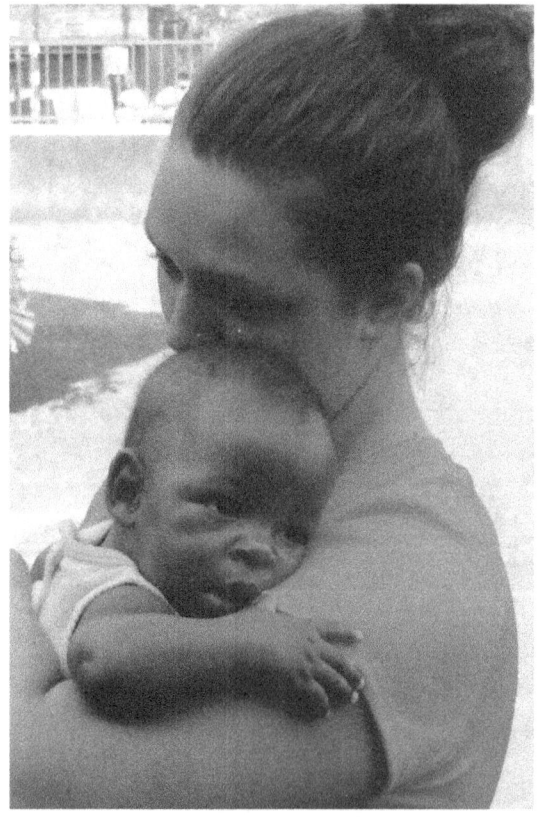

The yellow containers were lined up waiting to be filled with water in one of the villages. I do believe our granddaughter held every baby and child she could and would have stayed in Uganda if we had let her.

AOET started an elementary school where desks were greatly needed. Pictures of our early trip showed three students at one desk! A high school and several homes have since been added, and we visited them during my second trip.

Students at AOET School

Ugandan students sponsored by individuals primarily in the U.S. can now continue through high school; postsecondary education is being provided for many.

Red Feather Build

Several years ago, our son, knowing my passion, gave me a most wonderful Christmas present. He arranged for me to accompany him and his young son (our grandson) on a Red Feather build to the Turtle Mountain Reservation on the North Dakota/Canada border. Red Feather Development is a nonprofit organization that partners with indigenous communities to develop and implement lasting and impactful housing and building solutions.

My son, grandson, and I spent a week working with volunteers from around the country to build a straw bale construction ecology building for Turtle Mountain Community College. We slept in tents beside a beautiful lake and woke up every morning to the sounds of a variety of waterfowl on the lake.

The walls of the ecology building were stacked and secured with clean straw bales, which were wrapped with chicken wire and then mudded to look like stucco when the exterior was completed. The interior walls were natural pecan wood panels, which we oiled. All lighting was LED.

Our grandson had the opportunity to try all manner of tools and jobs. His tool belt was heavier than he was! One evening, we were guests of the college administration for a delicious dinner. Another evening, we had a big campfire near the lake with our group.

Though it sounds a bit bizarre, research and history show that straw bale buildings last for centuries and don't require the cutting down of trees for walls. Interestingly, the Taos Pueblos, which have lasted for centuries, are mud and grasses or straw mixed together to form hardened bricks and then mudded again on the sides. Straw bales were not yet available.

Both Taos Pueblo and Turtle Mountain Community College have utilized sustainable and environmentally sound construction methods. Built 1000+ years later, the ecology building is very modern-looking. To share the Red Feather experience with my son and grandson was an incredible blessing.

Women for the World

A few years ago, when I was still in Virginia, the issue of human trafficking came into the spotlight. My daughter had given me a copy of *Half the Sky* by Nicholas Kristof and Sheryl WuDunn, which details the oppression of women in southeast Asia, India, Pakistan, and several African countries—young girls who were abused, then considered unclean, and sold into prostitution; young girls forced to marry too young, delivering babies from immature bodies, damaged forever during delivery. Women and children were without rights or protections.

Some time later, I realized these horrors—very similar abuses—were literally happening in the United States, in my own community, and I was oblivious to them. Human trafficking, a form of slavery, generally falls into two categories: sexual exploitation and forced labor. Human trafficking can, of course, include the exploitation of men, though the preponderance of victims are women and children of both sexes.

What had likely been there for some time seemed to have exploded, with both men and women being used for sex trafficking and basically slave labor. Children aging out of the foster care system, who have few if any resources for survival and extremely limited support of any kind, seemed to be targets for traffickers, who promised them a place to stay and food. At the time, there was no organized effort to confront the problem.

In a moment of compassion, I pulled together a group of very capable young women and formed a nonprofit organization, Women for the World (W4TW). We held an organizational meeting halfway between Virginia and the Midwest, where some of the women lived. We agreed that our first project would be a focus on educating the public on human trafficking.

An open discussion with NOVA's college president and executive vice president jump-started the initiative at NOVA. Those of us at the college spent time working with other departments to bring the issue into the open.

At the time, some staff from other departments thought I was being a bit dramatic when I suggested that traffickers might well bring their victims to the college to apply for financial aid, as well. Why wouldn't they? The traffickers controlled their victims, maximum loans could be taken in the name of the victim, and the excess beyond minimum college costs would go into the pocket of the trafficker, who never had to repay a cent. Traffickers typically take all identification documents from their victims. Red flags would be "fathers" holding all identifying information for their "students." This actually happened.

The Virginia Association of Student Financial Aid Administrators (VASFAA) kicked off its 50th year at the 2017 conference. VASFAA annually supports a charity in the area of the state conference. As a VASFAA Board member and conference chair in 2017, I asked that we find a charity in the Virginia Beach area that assisted victims of abuse and human trafficking.

The YWCA of South Hampton Roads quickly rose to the surface to become our 2017 VASFAA Conference charity. Two of their staff members spoke to our group. We provided statistics and a quiz on human trafficking for conference attendees and collected donations for the YWCA. One of the true/false statements on the 15-question quiz was the following:

> Estimates indicate that human trafficking today (2017) is at 50% of the numbers trafficked at the height of the Atlantic slave trade.

That statement is false. When the last boat carried slaves for the Atlantic slave trade, estimates have total slaves in the Americas, Asia, and Africa (the biggest offenders) at about 24.5 million. There are an estimated 27-30 million people being trafficked in the world in 2017. (After the illegal sale of guns and drugs, human trafficking is the most profitable "business" in the world, and the second fastest growing. Every single one of the 22 high schools in Fairfax County, where I lived, had at the time experienced human trafficking.)

We asked attendees to take the message back to their schools and train staff members to recognize the signs of human trafficking. We subsequently spread the word to almost every postsecondary institution in Virginia.

Though W4TW made a difference by educating others and later moved into other areas of need, it wasn't long until secretaries of state across the country honed in on human trafficking and began trying to educate and recruit businesses to assist in prevention. I know hotel chains like Marriott have trained on human trafficking awareness for some years. Traffickers tend to move victims every few days to stay ahead of security and always know where demand is high. Big sporting events are just some of those areas.

Human Trafficking Hotline: 888-373-7888

As I write this, I am considering disbanding Women for the World. It served its purpose. Many of the projects we would now support are also nonprofit organizations, which would make gifts tax-deductible anyway. Tax deductibility is not the primary focus, but it does help limited funds go farther.

I have never solicited funding for W4TW and find that the number of solicitations I personally receive from other organizations on a daily basis is overwhelming. I will continue to support other organizations as I am able, but I strongly encourage everyone, before making a donation, to check charities for the percentage of funds that actually support the intended use and not administration. Some are just not in it for the right reasons! Women for the World never used one cent for administrative costs. It was a wonderful experience, but one that no longer seems necessary. Knowing when to stop is also valuable.

CHAPTER EIGHT

LIRA, A CHAPTER OF ITS OWN

Crested Crane, the National Bird of Uganda

Earlier in this book, I mentioned providing Alternatives to Violence workshops in northern Uganda, where the Lord's Resistance Army was still active. On the first trip in 2006, two young men from the Aids Orphans Education Trust, Jean, and I traveled west by van to Kampala and then north to Lira, a drive of several hours.

North of Kampala, a log was across the road. A bus headed toward us had been stopped by some men, whom I could only hope and pray had a legitimate purpose.

Rather than also stopping, our young driver went around the log and into the desert to continue on our way without explaining anything.

As we drove north, I realized we were in the area known as the killing fields, where thousands of skulls had been found following Idi Amin's reign of terror.

Upon our arrival in Lira, we located our hotel, which was a series of clean but sparsely furnished concrete rooms surrounding an enclosed plaza area where we had our meals. The next day, I facilitated an AVP workshop, with attendees being the mayor, city council members, and a few schoolteachers.

The following day was a workshop with orphaned children. I was literally on the verge of tears many times, but somehow managed to keep my emotions intact. So many children had lost parents—mostly to AIDS, but some to violence.

AOET employed a woman in Lira who was their contact there. I learned that there was a refugee camp a few miles outside Lira and asked if she would arrange for us to visit the camp. Though difficult for us to imagine the fear that drove them to the camp with its squalid conditions, the residents who fled there believed the camp to be safer from the LRA than their villages. Our AOET contact agreed to take us there.

The floor of the tent in the picture was filled with the sick and infirm. Camp refugees were of all ages and conditions, and those not in the tent used for the sick were living in all manner of makeshift huts.

Children followed us through the camp.

The camp appeared to be about the size of two football fields and held hundreds—possibly thousands—of men, women, and children packed together in makeshift hovels. We walked through a large, threadbare tent, which had been donated by a relief organization. Sick people were everywhere on pallets. We then walked among the shelters made of whatever could be scavenged and soon had dozens of little children following us.

One of the young men traveling with us was like the Pied Piper, and the children were smiling and giggling as he took their pictures. Our camp guide was an older gentleman who was referred to as the camp secretary. He took us into a chicken house that was locked up tighter than a drum to keep the donated chicks from being stolen. I never figured out how that number of chickens could supply eggs or meat to even a fraction of the refugees, or which refugees would be so privileged, but I guess something is better than nothing.

I had a small fanny pack, which contained my passport and a small amount of Ugandan currency. The thought occurred to me later that I was likely carrying more money than the people here had seen in their lifetimes. At the time, the average Ugandan income was just over the equivalent of $600 per year—for those who could work.

It wasn't until much later that I realized we could all have been killed for whatever we had, and no one would have ever known the difference. Strangely, I didn't once feel threatened or frightened by the people living in the camp.

As we walked along, I noticed young men on bicycles suddenly appearing in a circle surrounding us a short distance outside our small group. They wore nice dress shirts in various shades of bright blue. I quietly asked our guide who they were.

He nodded toward a large house that sat off the edge of the camp and whispered, "They live over there." Nothing else was volunteered, and I felt he was very uncomfortable having them around. We were obviously being watched but were never approached by them.

By the time we left the camp, it was dark. By the headlights of our van, I took a picture of the children standing by the fence watching us leave. Why weren't we taking them with us? The image has been etched in my mind all these years—complete with a lump in my throat.

When we got back to our hotel, two vans were in the parking area; their occupants were in the plaza. We learned the travelers were from the United Nations. Being a bit brazen and greatly impacted by the day's experiences, I walked up to one of the women who seemed to be an authority, introduced myself, and asked why more wasn't being done to assist the refugees in the camp.

She said there just wasn't enough money, and the camp was close enough to Lira that individuals could walk into town to work. I learned from others that "work" was sorting garbage for 7 cents a day! The woman gave me her card; I had just met the High Commissioner for Human Rights of the United Nations! I left the card with the head of AOET in hopes that he could help influence change for the refugees. I so wish I had kept it.

That night, as Jean and I were preparing for a restless sleep, we heard trucks rolling by and, at one point, heard gunshots. Strangely, we were more curious about what was happening than fearful for our lives.

The next morning, one of the young men with us came to tell us that we were supposed to immediately return to Bugembe without doing the last workshop. No explanation followed. On the drive east and then south, not the way we had come, we passed an army encampment of dugout shelters, which we were told could not be photographed. Before turning back west toward Bugembe, we came within a few miles of Kenya, a country I would still love to visit. Long before we reached the AOET compound, it was dark.

The whole experience seems surreal now, but we were stopped at least three times by armed soldiers who shone their lights into the van, looking for I don't know what. We sat quietly, were finally allowed to pass, and went on our way, not understanding whether this was the norm or an unusual occurrence. No one at AOET ever explained why we were called back. More on this later.

Switching to the Beauty of Uganda

On one afternoon while in Uganda, we were given the option to raft on the incredible Nile, which I did, and even swam in it. The area where we swam had more rapidly flowing water, which hippos and crocodiles don't like.

WELCOME TO THE SOURCE OF THE GREAT RIVER NILE - JINJA, UGANDA

JINJA MUNICIPAL COUNCIL

You are now at the Eastern bank of the River Nile, at a point where the river begins to flow from Lake Victoria (Source of the Nile) to the Mediterranean Sea. It takes water three months to complete this journey of 4000 miles (6400 km).

The falls that John Hannington Speke saw in 1862, naming them the "Ripon Falls" after the President of the Royal Geographical Society in London, submerged in 1947 on the construction of the giant Owen Falls Dam. The dam completed in 1954, harnesses the head long rush of water from the lake to produce hydro electric power for Uganda.

"Omugga Kiyira" is the local name for River Nile. The bay behind this bill board through which the waters of Lake Victoria funnel in the Nile is called Napoleon Gulf.

On the western bank of the river is an obelisk marking the spot where Speke stood for hours

After each trip to Uganda, travelers are also offered the opportunity to go on safari. We drove west from Kampala, stopped at the equator for pictures, and then headed on to Queen Elizabeth National Park.

Along the way, we passed large tea plantations, where pickers with bags over their shoulders picked the leaves. I asked why one individual was so far ahead of the others. We were told he was the "beater." His job was to beat the bushes to scare the snakes away before the pickers reached those bushes!

Mweya Safari Lodge, located in Queen Elizabeth, is a beautiful facility that sits high on a ridge overlooking the Kazinga Channel, which connects Lakes Edward and George, part of the African Great Lakes system. The Kazinga Channel is home to the largest population of hippos anywhere in the world. We took a boat tour and saw them up close.

We even saw a baby hippo nursing underwater, a feat of which I was unaware. The first evening, I saw a group of travelers looking over the side of a little gazebo area, and I walked down to see what they were so excited about. A hippo was grazing right outside the railing. We also learned on this trip that more deaths occur from hippos than from any other African animal. Their jaws are deadly.

One night, we heard some serious squealing and asked at breakfast what it might have been. Apparently, a pride of lions lived near the lodge, and a lion had likely gotten a warthog. Yes, we were told not to walk around at night! The thought also occurred to me that the bacon we were served at the lodge was warthog. I didn't see any Iowa-type porkers over there!

On the first safari, we were able to spot lions eating on a kob. There seemed to be two lionesses with cubs who were hierarchically taking turns chowing down. What was interesting was that other kobs had formed a loose circle out quite a distance from the lions, watching their comrade become lunch—a perfect example of keeping your friends close and your enemies closer!

We saw many elephants and babies on this safari. One of our drivers asked if we wanted to stay out after dark one night to try to find big cats, especially leopards. As we were going around a curve, a huge bull elephant was walking down the sandy trail right toward us. Our driver quickly put the safari wagon in reverse and began backing up. The elephant just kept coming.

At one point, the driver tried to make a jackknife turn to drive away, but couldn't get it done fast enough. He changed his mind, and we kept backing up with the elephant headed toward us. If he had hit us sideways, we would surely have tipped over. After what seemed like at least a half mile, the bull finally tired and walked off the road through the grass.

I wasn't able to return to Uganda until 2013. This time, our grand-daughter Jesse and one of my coworkers accompanied me on the trip. I was again asked to go to Lira, this time to facilitate an AVP workshop for parents of the new school that AOET had recently built in the country outside Lira.

During their time of terror, the LRA had kidnapped villagers and/or recruited others to work with them. When someone escaped from the LRA or returned to the village, as some did, distrust was rampant—and understandably so. AOET wanted me to attempt to help build community for the school. Team building, communication, and creative conflict resolution are the tenets of AVP.

The school building was packed to the point where there was no opportunity for the usual AVP exercises that required movement, but we made it work. At the end of the workshop, participants formed a large circle, and I went from person to person, greeting each one and thanking them for coming.

One older lady proudly told me that she was the oldest person in her village. She was 56 years old! She could have passed for 75 and was younger than I by over a decade! I encouraged her, and now I wonder if she could possibly still be living. Long life has a different definition and expectation in Uganda. I was given the morning for the workshop, but was told later that the participants stayed around for some time, wanting more workshop interaction, a new concept for most, if not all, of them. I would gladly have stayed longer had I known.

After this trip, we again went to Queen Elizabeth National Park. On this trip, park rangers asked if we wanted to accompany them at night to a spot where they were going to call in hyenas so they could tag them. They used the sound of a dying animal to try to lure the hyenas closer.

After waiting for several hours, the rangers said it didn't look like they would be successful, and we might as well go back to the lodge. As we were driving down this dark, one-lane, sandy road, our headlights beamed on an animal lying in the road. It appeared to be injured. Some of us wondered if we should help it.

The driver quickly said to stay in the safari vehicle, which had open sides about three feet above shoulder height when seated. He left his headlights on and shut off the engine. It wasn't long before another animal came out of the grass—then another and another until six very large hyenas, including the one playing dead, began to investigate the intruders into their territory. They moved slowly and began circling the van. I suddenly found myself looking out the open space into the huge face of a very ferocious-looking hyena, with my granddaughter behind me in the back seat!

At that point, I remember saying, "Okay, time to go. Time to go!" I didn't know whether that big guy could jump or not, but I knew none of us would win a battle with those jaws. He was one scary creature—and I looked like dinner!

Mweya Safari Lodge is lovely and has a small pool that felt mighty refreshing on a hot afternoon. As my granddaughter, a staff member, and a few others were enjoying the lounge chairs and water, one of the lodge staff members came by to ask if we wanted anything.

A sudden small scream was the precursor to his rapid departure, which we didn't understand until we saw movement under a nearby lounge chair. Pulling out my phone, I took a picture of a beautiful, shiny green snake that posed with its head up in cobra fashion.

Paul had previously told me of his encounter with a black mamba (actually grey to dark brown in color), an incredibly fast and highly venomous snake, from which he escaped without being bitten. The snake we encountered was definitely bright green, and although it acted a bit like a cobra, it did not have that appearance.

Much later, we learned why the young lodge employee fled so rapidly, but wished he had told us. We were in the presence of a green mamba, a fast-moving and highly venomous snake that I didn't even know existed. Leaving the pool ...

Having gone on three different safaris on three trips to Africa, I feel so incredibly fortunate to have seen such a variety of beautiful animals in their habitats. Each safari was different and memorable beyond belief. Even at the lodge, we were invading the animals' territory.

I recently read *The Ministry for the Future*, a fiction/non-fiction book about global warming and its ramifications. The author, Kim Stanley Robinson, brings the concept of Half the World into the storyline.

The Half the World concept returns half the world to nonhuman animals, restoring native areas and providing safe crossings in areas inhabited by humans. After seeing such majestic animals restricted to park areas for survival, I appreciate the perspective and wonder how we could make it happen.

Every year, more species move dangerously close to extinction. Not unlike ranchers with livestock close to Yellowstone National Park, villagers close to Queen Elizabeth suffer when they lose livestock due to large predators, though they aren't supposed to have livestock that close.

While we were there, a lion had killed a villager's cow. The villagers found and poisoned the carcass so the lions would be poisoned when they returned for another meal. Unfortunately, lions are deemed the enemy, though they are simply doing what lions do, and their numbers have greatly diminished.

Because the visit to the refugee camp on my first trip was so impactful, I inquired about the camp as soon as we arrived back in Lira on the second trip and asked to go there. I was told it was no longer there. I was excited and asked if that meant the refugees were able to return to their villages. Again, I was told the camp was no longer there … no further explanation.

After asking multiple people, the new AOET contact in Lira drove me to a spot that was supposedly the camp. I said this location was so small and looked nothing like the one I visited. She quietly replied, "Oh, you must have gone to the other camp." She also told me that when she first went to Lira, she hid under her bed every time she heard gunfire. After much probing of others, I finally learned what happened.

The story, as I know it to be:

One night, there was an attempt to empty the refugee camp—by whom, I don't know for sure—presumably to send those living there back to their villages. They were deemed a problem for the city. Someone started shooting. An estimated 300-400 men, women, and children were killed. I was told the only thing remaining now at that refugee camp site is a huge V-shaped mass grave. The people of the area were told they were never to speak of it. No one would take me there.

To my knowledge, there was nothing in the news or "history books" about the mass killing. Apparently, the victims weren't important, and the massacre was too embarrassing. I eventually saw two small signs in obscure areas of Lira indicating the tragedy, but the year on the signs had to be wrong because it was well before the date of our first trip when we visited the camp.

Upon our return to Bugembe on that second trip, I shared what I had learned in Lira with our group back at the AOET compound. Jean, especially, was heartbroken, as I had been. We both remembered the faces of the many children in the camp and knew the victims had to have included the very young and infirm. To this day, I wonder if the massacre happened the very night before we quite unexpectedly left Lira on our first trip. I can't help but feel that it did.

On this second trip to Uganda, I saw that the U.S. military had a presence there. The United States and Uganda have tried without success to capture Joseph Kony, founder and leader of the Lord's Resistance Army. He has been reported in southern Sudan, the Democratic Republic of Congo, and the Central African Republic.

Though his influence is less visible and seems to have diminished over time, he is responsible for the kidnapping of thousands of children who were turned into soldiers or sex slaves, and for displacing an estimated two million people. In 2005, he was indicted for war crimes and crimes against humanity by the International Criminal Court (ICC) in The Hague, but he has evaded capture.

CHAPTER NINE

THE PENDULUM THEORY

Whether I read this, heard this, or simply developed this concept through the years, I'm unsure. An experience I had as an 18-year-old demonstrates it well.

I was renewing my driver's license for the first time, only to remember the deadline after coming home from college for winter break and realizing that the courthouse department I normally used was open only on certain days and would not be open again prior to the holidays or my birthday.

My sister went with me, and we drove to a neighboring county so I could renew my license. At that time, the highway we were traveling on had slanted curbing along both sides, likely a throwback to days of much smaller vehicles. I accidentally hit the curb on the right and was thrown left. I then hit the opposite side and began careening down the road, shifting from right to left, never finding the middle of the road.

Fortunately, it was a slow day on this rural highway! It wasn't long until my sister, who was older—and presumably wiser—yanked the wheel to the right and we slid on the car's side down the right-side ditch on a snowbank.

Rather unbelievably, no one was injured, the car did not have a scratch on it, and a very helpful farmer came by and drove the car out of the ditch to a side road. My somewhat limited driving experience had resulted in overcorrecting multiple times, but I was somehow able to drive on and renew my license.

What seems to happen way too frequently in our country is overcorrecting, and the swinging of the pendulum begins. It happens in many areas of life, especially in major decisions that attempt to solve societal problems. In the only country founded on the principle that we could and should govern ourselves, we struggle to make sound and consistent decisions.

The majority opinion creates a plan that may be too bold to begin with. When it doesn't work, we tend to swing drastically in the other direction and overcorrect. When that doesn't work, we swing back in the opposite direction and overcorrect once again.

Often, as in conflict resolution scenarios, the sense is that there isn't enough of some resource, including money, to go around, or that a decision gives power or resources to the "few" or the "wrong" group. The process tends to repeat ad nauseam because each "side" is convinced they are "right," the discourse becomes heated, and we can't seem to find the middle of the road!

We don't have to compromise on a decision that is less than our best, but we certainly need to collaborate to find the best decision that is sustainable and long-lasting. Way too frequently, the answers are somewhere in the middle, but those making the decisions are too stubborn to admit that the opposing views might have some merit. This might be the place for another favorite saying by Harry S. Truman: "We would be amazed at what we could accomplish if it didn't matter who gets the credit."

We are currently experiencing one of those swings in 2025, following the change in governmental administrations. Just one example: Whereas the previous administration viewed DEI, environmental issues, and prejudices against individuals self-designating as LGBTQ+ as societal issues that needed to be addressed, the new administration is eliminating all support for said focuses. Pretending issues don't exist is not an answer.

M.K. Gandhi said, "It is the reformer who is anxious for the reform, and not society, from which he should expect nothing better than opposition, abhorrence, and even mortal persecution. Why may not society regard as retrogression what the reformer holds dear as life itself?"

George Orwell provides additional insight. "The further a society drifts from the truth, the more it will hate those who speak it."

CHAPTER TEN

GROUNDED IN FAITH

I would not be honest if I didn't bring my faith into the conversation. I grew up in a family with several generations of Christian tradition. My maternal great-grandfather was a minister—Lutheran, I believe— and one of the signers who founded a Christian college in Illinois on his way west by covered wagon.

As an adult, whenever I visited my maternal grandmother, I would find her at the dining room table, reading her Bible. She never tried to push her faith on any of us, though I loved to visit Sunday School and church when we were visiting Grandma. When asked to which church she belonged, she always responded, "I am a member at the Methodist Church, but I belong to God's church." Grandma was a truly devout woman and lived her faith.

I grew up Methodist, so church with Grandma was familiar and expected. Some years after I reached adulthood, I realized that my dad most likely grew up in a more conservative church. He didn't believe in dancing ("vertical fulfillment for horizontal desires") and only had a beer when his brothers-in-law or sons handed him one. He sprinkled salt in it and drank it so fast that I don't think he even tasted it!

One of Dad's school supplies salesmen gave him a bottle of whiskey for Christmas. It stayed on a very high shelf in our kitchen cupboards and only came down when one of us kids had the croup. Dad would put a few drops of whiskey on a spoonful of sugar for us to take. "A spoonful of sugar helps the 'medicine' go down!" Amazingly, the concoction seemed to work and probably helped us fall asleep!

Dad was a very caring, yet not demonstrative, person. When he was in the final few weeks of his battle with esophageal cancer, I visited him for a week from Montana. I told him I loved him and wished I could take the pain from him. His response was, "I love all you kids." I knew he did, but I don't ever remember him telling me that directly.

Just recently, my sister told me that one of the boys who was in school with us came to her at a class or school reunion recently and told her that Dad had saved their lives. That was confusing until he explained. They were an exceptionally poor family with several children, living in very substandard housing. He said Dad used to bring food to their house. None of us had any idea, and Dad would never have told anyone. He lived his faith. I also well remember Dad saying, "If you can't say anything nice, say nothing."

From the choirs I directed, the youth groups I led, the Mission Committee, the choir in which I sang, and the years of weekly attendance at church, you might have gathered that I am a believer—and I am. For years, "Footprints in the Sand," written by Mary Stevenson in 1936, has given me comfort and hope. The poem reminds us of God's presence in our lives during the most difficult times, even when we feel we are walking all alone.

But that is only part of the story …

I recently read a quote that said, "Religion requires faith, but faith does not require religion." I have felt that way for some time. It started many years ago.

In the era when I was in high school, Protestants and Catholics did not date. Catholic families had no church choice in my community and went to one of two neighboring towns for church.

When one of those small towns, which was almost exclusively Catholic, closed its Catholic school and came to the one I attended, we were all friends, but dating rules were unwritten, understood, and gradually eroded. When John F. Kennedy ran for President, his Catholic faith was a huge issue in the election, much like Mormonism became an issue when Mitt Romney ran for President in 2016.

Until recently, I didn't know that the first Latter Day Saint (Mormon) to run for President was Joseph Smith, who was also the first American presidential candidate to be assassinated (June 27, 1844) with his brother, Hiram, near Nauvoo, Illinois, right across the Mississippi, not far from Fort Madison, Iowa.

I also recently learned that a group of Mormons broke away from Brigham Young, the new Mormon leader, as he led followers across Iowa and on to Salt Lake. Those who stayed in Iowa didn't believe in polygamy and developed a town a very short distance from where I grew up. The community had 30-40 families, a school, and a church at one time.

When the railroad bypassed Manti, the Mormon community, and was built several miles away, most of the residents moved to Shenandoah to be close to the railroad and a more thriving economy. We had elementary school outings to Manti, now a protected historic area where only the house of the leader and a cemetery remain, but I never fully understood the history.

When I worked as the Financial Aid Director at my first college, a Christian college affiliated with Christian Churches, students came to my office regularly. Possibly because they were already sharing so much to qualify for financial aid, I quickly learned that many of our students arrived at school with more baggage than any person should experience in an entire lifetime. Students shared so much with me that I chose to get my master's in higher education counseling so I would know better how to respond without hurting them.

One student provided my first discussion with a young man who was gay. He was dating a lovely young woman at the time and was very confused. Another student had been sexually abused from early childhood—by her father—and was having horrible nightmares that she couldn't understand. She eventually went into a residential facility for assistance, worked through the trauma, married, and had a lovely family of her own.

I felt we had a number of students coming to the college as a safe place where others would care, and I was honored that they trusted me. Imagine the hurt felt by gay students and my disappointment in the college when homosexuality was simply not acceptable. It was considered a sin and treated like alcoholism, which simply meant, "Don't imbibe."

My office was next door to a classroom where the pastoral ministries professor taught pastoral ministry majors. I was seated in my office one day with my door and the classroom door both open. I heard the instructor telling his students that he had been asked to fill the pulpit at the congregational church in the country, a sister church to the one we were attending in town at that time. He told them how much he enjoyed it and how nice the people were. Then he added, "But I don't know … on the day of judgment … they haven't been immersed."

I had been allowed to lead a student group, the only woman at the college to do so. As stated previously, women were not to teach men when men reached puberty. I didn't know this, but was told by other women at the college who were not allowed to lead student groups. To this day, I don't know why I was an exception.

I had also started a prison ministry and a summer mission program—and basically had just been told by the ministry professor that I was going to hell because my baptism had not been by immersion! Not long thereafter, I was asked to apply for the Director's position at a four-year public college, was offered the job, and made the decision to take it. I truly regretted leaving the students with whom I had become close, but I was able to maintain a relationship with both of the aforementioned students and several others who most needed support.

As an adult, I attended Protestant churches—Methodist, Congregational, Presbyterian—and literally felt little, if any, difference in the services. While in Virginia, we began attending a wonderful Presbyterian church where I began singing in the choir, the most incredible church choir I have ever heard. The Director was professionally trained but had never joined that Presbyterian church after many years as the Director.

His adult son told me that his family had dinner after church each Sunday and discussed what parts of the sermon were accurate and which were not. They came from a very conservative faith, as well, and apparently loved the choir but didn't embrace the theology, which I found disconcerting.

Our choir had about 30 members who sang each Sunday, six to eight of whom could have been or did sing professionally. None were paid to sing in our choir. The music we sang was wonderfully challenging, and we normally had a special high-level musical event in early summer—often not of religious origin—and a beautiful Christmas music service on the first or second Sunday in December. I LOVED singing with this choir!

The evening after our morning Christmas service was typically our time for a holiday choir party at the beautiful home of a couple who both sang in the choir. Members brought hors d'oeuvres and wine; we ordered Chinese food, and then had a Christmas hymn and carol sing after dinner.

Our organist, who was also the organist for a major university, and her husband, who had a military background in Germany, brought Glüh-wein, a hot German wine. As I was drinking a glass of wine and filling my plate, the Director, who was right behind me, said, "Real Christians don't drink wine."

I said, "What?! What DID Jesus serve at the Last Supper?"

He replied, "Grape juice."

And I asked, "And the first miracle? Jesus turned water into what at the wedding feast?"

Again, he replied, "Grape juice."

I was leaving for Iowa the next morning, but had planned to stay for the songfest. After dinner, I thanked our host and hostess, got my coat, and left. Even after church members called on me, I never went back to choir or church after I returned from the holidays.

As I was driving from Virginia to Iowa, I passed through a small town in Pennsylvania, which appeared to have a population of around 1,000 people, from the looks of it. On the edge of town was a huge board that listed 12 to 16 different churches with the times of their worship services. As I looked at it, my only thought was, "And they all think they are right." The town I live in now has SO many churches, and I'm confident they all think they are "right" too.

Our financial aid staff in Virginia was reflective of the diversity in the area. I never measured it in numbers, as it just didn't matter, but we had a very diverse staff in terms of age, gender, race, ethnicity, and reli-gion. Several key positions were held by Muslims, who have all been labeled by some in our country as Jihadists and a threat to Christians. Like any other trusted colleagues and friends, I would have put my life in their hands.

I have said to myself and a few others through the years that if we had a church for everyone's personal beliefs, we might need one for each of us. I don't need to hate someone for believing differently than I do. In fact, I think I can learn something from each—perhaps one more piece of the puzzle. I have come to believe that no religion has a corner on all the good ideas.

Years ago, I read *Mutant Message Down Under* by Marlo Morgan. The message is presented as the true story of an American woman who was invited to a banquet in her honor, but to her surprise, found herself invited on a walkabout through the Australian outback. Some readers likely missed the point of her spiritual journey when they realized it was likely not a true story. I just wish I could have actually been there!

At one point, toward the end of the book, the woman asked tribal members if they had heard of Jesus. Yes, they had, but they continued by saying, "Jesus didn't come to us. We were already doing all those things."

I recently read that "light" in Hebrew means creating order out of chaos. Literally, I had a light bulb moment! When Jesus said, "I am the light of the world," was he asking to be worshipped—or was he asking to be heard? If we all follow his teachings—and those of other wise spiritual leaders—could we turn this chaotic world into an orderly and peaceful home?

I certainly don't have all the answers, but my faith is as strong as ever. I have had too many unexplainable experiences to believe there is not a greater being. I believe it was a priest in the movie *Rudy* who said, "In

my 35 years of religious studies, I have come up with only two incon-
trovertible facts:

- There is a God, and
- I am not Him."

As Dr. Lueninghoener, my college geology professor and the man for
whom the Midland planetarium is named, said years ago, "The pieces
of an intricate watch are not just put in a hat and shaken to become a
watch. They need a designing hand." Even if you are a believer in the
Big Bang theory, who created the materials and who lit the fuse?

Religion has been the source of more conflicts and wars than you or I
can count. I mentioned earlier that I recently read Mark Twain's book,
Joan of Arc. Since much of the book was a translation from French history, I must believe it is as accurate an interpretation of what actually
happened as any could be.

For years, I—for whatever reason—believed Joan was burned at the
stake by the very country she had saved from the English. The book
clearly indicates she was executed by the church, justified "through her
wickedness, a menace and peril to the church's purity and holiness, her
death therefore necessary." The church abandoned her after she saved
the country!

In Twain's Appendix to the book, he reviews Joan of Arc's incredible
life. She was deeply religious. Without training or education and at
the age of 17, she led armies that led to the English being driven out
of France after many years, while showing compassion to those she
fought.

As Twain stated, "Taking into account … her origin, youth, sex, illit-
eracy, early environment, and the obstructing conditions under which
she exploited her high gifts and made her conquests in the field and

before the courts that tried her for her life—she is easily and by far the most extraordinary person the human race has ever produced." Of all his writings, Mark Twain said, "I like *Joan of Arc* best of all my books; and it is the best ..."

I recently read *As Long as the Grass Shall Grow and Rivers Flow, A History of Native Americans* by Clifford E. Trafzer. Because the book is written by a native American, though heavily referencing many writers, the history is not at all what we learned in K-12 education. Though some missionaries and Indian agents respected Indian cultures and peoples, Indians were viewed as uncivilized savages who needed to be Christianized.

Many simply wanted Indians off the land and either destroyed or forced onto reservations, whose borders kept changing as more and more land was demanded by white settlers. (Don't get me started on David Grann's *Killers of the Flower Moon* ... unbelievable greed and evil! The current push to open public lands and even national parks to drilling and private use feels very much like another chapter in that book.)

Religious leaders—from Catholic to Puritan and beyond—were part of the devastation for tribes across the country. While working in Nebraska, I attended the Healing the Hoop Conference in Lincoln and heard amazing speakers, including Wilma Mankiller and N. Scott Momaday. Mr. Momaday signed the program for me. I believe it was Wilma Mankiller who began her presentation by saying, "My name is Wilma Mankiller. I am a recovering Catholic."

At the time, I was shocked, but learning more about the removal of Indian children from their homes and the forced education and indoctrination into the Catholic faith helped clarify her introduction and lifetime of pain. The model Jesus gave us was nowhere to be found.

Though a significant number of Indians have become Christians, white man's faith should never have been forced on them, and I tend to think we can still learn a great deal from the holistic approach to life that was the foundation of tribal culture and faith.

Judaism, Islam, and Christianity are all based on the Old Testament—and we diverge from there. I believe the Bible contains great messages for mankind, but it must be read and learned from in its entirety. Some believe that the Bible is the very words of God. That seems doubtful after many interpretations in many languages by individuals influenced by their cultures over many centuries. Perhaps the "word of God," but certainly not the very "words of God."

What I do know is that judging others, whether they be Catholic, Protestant, Jewish, Muslim, Buddhist, straight, LGBTQ+, or anything else, is way above my pay grade! Elected officials today seem to have forgotten why our country was built on the premise of the separation of church and state. Fear is rearing its ugly head. "Those who forget our history are doomed to repeat it."

Religion seems to be an attempt by humans to understand the universe and mitigate fear of the unknown. M.K. Gandhi, in his autobiography, tells of his struggles and "experiments with the truth" in trying to discern the way he should live.

Spiritual leaders around the world have said so many wise things that have been quoted, misquoted, interpreted, reinterpreted, misinterpreted—and locked into dogmas, rituals, and beliefs that pit one person against another, one community against another, one country against another, one so-called faith against another—all in an attempt to understand our world, our universe ... all in the name of God.

People are often unreasonable, illogical, and self-centered.
Forgive them anyway.
If you are kind, people may accuse you of selfish, ulterior motives.
Be kind anyway.
If you are successful, you will win some false friends and sometimes
true enemies.
Be successful anyway.
If you are honest and frank, people may cheat you.
Be honest and frank anyway.
What you spend years building, someone could destroy overnight.
Build anyway.
If you find serenity and happiness, they may be jealous.
Be happy anyway.
The good you do today, people will often forget tomorrow.
Do good anyway.
Give the world your best, and it may never be enough.
Give the world the best you have anyway.
You see, in the final analysis, it is between you and God.
It was never between you and them anyway.

... often attributed to Mother Teresa

"... between you and God," or whatever you call the supreme being, not between you and any form of religion.

In 2019, after double-checking with the state to ensure it was legal, I had the unexpected and beautiful honor and responsibility of officiating at our grandson's wedding. I will forever consider it one of the great privileges of my life.

Two short months later, the beloved daughter of my next-older sister died of ovarian cancer at 35 years of age. The Catholic church had basically deserted her when she had divorced her husband for cause some months earlier.

When the priest offered the last rites and finally allowed her communion, she couldn't take it because she was no longer able to swallow. I was the officiant for her large funeral, which was not in the church.

Most recently, our children and I planned my husband's/their father's memorial service. The Prayer of St. Francis was included in all three of these ceremonies. The wisdom herein is universal, has always spoken to me, and seems to be an all-encompassing roadmap for life. Though attributed to St. Francis, "religion" has no part in it.

Prayer of St. Francis

Lord, make me an instrument of Thy peace.

Where there is hatred, let me sow love;

Where there is injury, pardon;

Where there is doubt, faith;

Where there is despair, hope;

Where there is darkness, light;

Where there is sadness, joy.

O Divine Master, grant that I might not so much seek

to be consoled as to console;

To be understood as to understand;

To be loved as to love.

For it is in giving that we receive,

It is in pardoning that we are pardoned,

And it is in dying that we are born to eternal life.

CHAPTER ELEVEN

ISSUES OF UNITY AND DIVERSITY

Early in this book, I mentioned that I created and taught a course titled "Issues of Unity and Diversity." The influences to create that course were many. Having grown up in a small midwestern community of 500 Caucasian residents (498 until the Jack twins were born; then still Caucasian!), I knew something was missing.

I remember too well the first time I heard someone use the "N" word. I was in fourth grade. A sixth-grade girl, whom I still know, said she and her family had gone to Omaha, and she had seen an "N." Though I now know that she wouldn't have said that had she not been influenced by family, I can't see her without hearing that word.

When I was in junior high, my seventh- and eighth-grade English teacher gave me my first adult book to read, *Fair Oaks* by Frank Yerby. Considering that my dad was the superintendent, that was quite trusting of her. Set in the South, slavery and abuse were part of the story.

I then read the sequel, *Foxes of Harrow*. A year or two ago, I found and purchased *Fair Oaks* online and reread it. Ironically, Fair Oaks was the name of the area where I recently lived in northern Virginia, and I just learned that the town where I currently live in Iowa was first called "Fair Oaks" … very strange!

I recently reread two additional books that I read in college. *Five Smooth Stones* by Ann Fairburn is the story of a young black boy and a white girl who fell in love, forbidden at the time, and until 1967, when Loving vs. Virginia struck down state laws banning marriage between individuals of different races.

The second book, *Black Like Me* by John Howard Griffin, is the story of a white man who dyed his skin black and traveled through the South to experience what life was like as a black man. I bought *Black Like Me* after I heard Mr. Griffin speak at Conception Junction and Monastery in Missouri when I was in college. The book was extremely impactful, but Griffin could never fully experience what being black was like because he always had the option to again become white.

Books can add to the personal experiences that influence one's life. Keep in mind that these books were all written before the Civil Rights Act. The March on Washington occurred in the summer after I graduated from high school.

In September of that year, 1963, a Gallup poll showed that 52% of Americans who responded thought race relations or racism was the greatest problem facing the U.S. In May of 2020, after George Floyd's death, the result was still 19%. In January 2025, only 3% of responding Americans believed race relations/racism to be our *greatest* problem. That in no way means "problem solved" or that we no longer have racism.[14]

I know exactly where I was when John F. Kennedy was shot, and I've been to the memorial museum in Dallas. I remember well the killings of Bobby Kennedy and Martin Luther King Jr.

---

[14] Inc. Gallup, "Gallup Center on Black Voices," Gallup.com, July 15, 2020, https://news.gallup.com/315575/measuring-black-voices.aspx?utm_source=gallup_brand&utm_medium=email&utm_campaign=front_page_2_february_02112025&utm_term=information&utm_content=latest_from_gallup_center_on_black_voices_textlink_3.

A few years ago, when I was at a conference in Memphis, a staff member encouraged us to visit the Lorraine Motel, where MLK Jr. was shot. Another staff member and I walked to Ebenezer Baptist Church while in Atlanta for a meeting. Sitting in the sanctuary and hearing a recording of a MLK Jr. sermon was a spiritual experience. He was still there. Each of these experiences was emotional and impactful—an opportunity to learn and grow.

Another book that has greatly impacted me is *The Seven Daughters of Eve* by Bryan Sykes. Sykes is a renowned geneticist who, through researching mitochondrial DNA on human remains around the world, traced all humans back to seven women. Mitochondrial DNA was used because it mutates at a much lower rate than male DNA.

Since my mother was the only female in her family and is no longer living, my cousin, who has completed much of our family's genealogy, asked if my sisters or I would submit the test to see if she could make ancestral links back further. I was honestly surprised—and subsequently pleased—to find names from many ethnicities in my DNA. The path for humans begins in Africa and then spreads north, but I feel like I am a true citizen of the world and related to all. I love it!

I mentioned earlier in the book that my views on racism have been greatly impacted by my nephew. He was a three-year-old, beautiful little black boy adopted along with his beautiful five-year-old half-sister into my sister's white family in the early '70s after being with them as foster children.

Most people thought they were very fortunate children to have found a "white" family, which in many ways was true, but it wasn't because the family was white, and life wasn't always easy for the two children.

Because of my brother-in-law's work, the family moved from Des Moines to Dallas and then to Concord, California—all cities with a fair amount of diversity. One year, my nephew asked if he could bring his Boy Scout troop to our rural acreage in Montana on their way home to California from the World Scout Jamboree held that year in Calgary. A pretty sizable troop pitched their tents in our yard and stayed with us on their way home. It was such fun to host them and see my nephew so happy.

As my nephew became a teenager, his family left California and moved to a heavily Caucasian area of Wisconsin. My nephew never wanted to be black but couldn't be anything else—and shouldn't have felt the need to be.

At 17, he was dating a white girl who meant a great deal to him. Her parents thought it was getting too serious and told her she couldn't see him any longer; he was, after all, black. This beautiful, caring young man went home, somehow got a gun, and shot himself.

As ugly as much of our history is, it is unfortunately still our history. We can't just pretend it doesn't exist. "Those who don't learn from our history are doomed to repeat it."

By the time I became the Director of Financial Aid at my first community college, I felt the need to create a course that would help broaden the perspectives of students who had often never been out of the state or exposed to other races or cultures. At the time, the town of about 20,000 where I was living and working was still almost 100% Caucasian. As Bell Hooks says, "Teach in the radical spaces of possibility."

"Issues of Unity and Diversity," the course I created and taught, included four major concepts:

- Know yourself; you carry baggage.
- A little knowledge is a dangerous thing.
- People do things for their reasons, not ours.
- No culture has a corner on all the good ideas.

#1: Know yourself; you carry baggage.

We *all* do! We have been conditioned—socialized—to be biased. To some extent, we are all guilty of ethnocentrism, *believing, as a people group, that our own solutions in developing a culture are superior to any others and would be recognized as superior by any right-thinking, intelligent, logical human being.* Would it surprise you to know that ALL cultures likely feel that way? (If they didn't, they would change!)

Diversity is defined as race, gender, age, language, physical characteristics, disability, sexual orientation, economic status, parental status, education, geographic origin, profession, lifestyle, religion, position in the company hierarchy, and any other difference ... so *many possibilities for prejudice!*

Questions ... answers ... and clues:

- Have you ever told a joke that referenced someone from a group listed above?
- Have you ever listened to or allowed such a joke and said nothing?
- Have you ever felt that entire people groups were the cause of their own problems?
- Have you ever felt that other religions were just *wrong*—or lifestyles—or orientations?
- Are you uncomfortable in the presence of individuals who are *different* from you?

Have you ever just *known* that others speaking a different language in your presence are talking about you? (*What makes you think you are important enough for them to be discussing you?*)

We have been socially conditioned to be biased:

- To think one is immune may be the height of naivete or arrogance.

- Bias and prejudice are learned behaviors.
- We can grow and change if we are personally willing to confront and unlearn prejudicial conditioning.
- Unlearning our biases means acquiring accurate information and experiences.

Every bigot was once a child free from prejudice!

To paraphrase Jack Gordon (1992), managing diversity means:

Developing a system and a culture that unite different people in a common pursuit without undermining their diversity. It is achieving "unum" without asking the "pluribus" to do quite so much melting.[15]

Instead of a melting pot where we must all blend together and blend in, why not consider us a tossed salad where each of us maintains our unique characteristics, but when mixed together, yields a "flavor" that is superior to any single one of us?

Per Steven Covey, the goal is synergy—building a culture and environment that is so much greater than the sum of its parts—by valuing, embracing, and not fearing the differences. Building that culture, whether in the workplace or community, begins with each one of us. *We have work to do, starting with "the man in the mirror."*

#2: A little knowledge is a dangerous thing.

Unfortunately, human beings tend to take the knowledge they/we have learned from meeting one or a few individuals from another culture and attribute that knowledge and the characteristics of those few people to an entire people group. In other words, we stereotype! There are actually more differences within a people group than there are between people groups.

---

[15] Jack Gordon, "Rethinking Diversity," Training, November 30, 1991, https://eric.ed.gov/?q =about&pg=11241&id=EJ437113.

I remember reading a story years ago about a common-looking couple who visited one of the Ivy League colleges to inquire about creating a faculty chair in memory of their son. The Dean of the college appraised them as a well-meaning but uninformed couple who couldn't possibly fund such an endeavor.

As the couple was being summarily dismissed, they asked what it would cost to create an entire university in another part of the country. When given the figure as they walked out, the wife said, "We could do that, couldn't we?" To the Dean's dismay, some months later, the couple established Stanford University in memory of their son.

My "Issues of Unity and Diversity" class required open discussion and sharing. In one of the early sections, we were discussing racial issues and stereotypes. A young woman opened up about her dad's literal hatred of all black individuals. She went on to explain that when her dad was in the service, a black man held a gun to his head. After confirming that he had endured a very frightening experience, I asked, "Do you think your dad would hate all white people if a white man had held a gun to his head?"

Globalization has opened new and unique ways and channels for the media and people around the world to communicate and exchange ideas and news with each other. One of the essential advantages of this process is the integration of people, nations, organizations, and institutions from various parts of the world with various individual and organizational cultures. The downside would be accessing only channels of information that purposefully create negativity and further enhance stereotyping.

Cities are more diverse and neighborhoods look different; daily, we encounter many people from different ethnic, racial, and religious backgrounds. Cities often resemble crowded terminals at international airports—like in Dubai, Frankfurt, or London.

But our cities *are not* airport terminals where people wait for airplanes to take them back home. Most people around us are here permanently. There is no plane waiting to take them home because this is **HOME!** In the 2020 census, approximately 42.2% of the U.S. population reported their race and ethnicity as something other than non-Hispanic white alone, an increase from one-third in the 2010 census. We are an increasingly diverse country. Some fear that will mean a loss of power and control.

All of us, at one time or another, were immigrants or descendants of immigrants to this land. When we were living in Montana, I remember hearing often, "I'm here now; close the gates!" Those new to the state selfishly wanted to limit access by others who wanted the same beauty and spaciousness offered by the glory that is Montana.

If diversity is part of American culture—if not American culture itself—why do we know so little about one another?

- Is it due to limited knowledge that so often creates negative stereotypes and fear of new cultures?
- Is it the limited or sometimes absolute absence of interest in one another?
- Or is it just fear that learning about others might change us and challenge our individual cultures?

A little learning is a dangerous thing …

> *"While from the bounded level of our mind, Short views we take*
> *nor see the lengths behind, But more advanced behold with strange*
> *surprise, New distant scenes of endless science rise!"*
> —Alexander Pope[16]

---

[16] By, "12 of the Best Alexander Pope Quotations," Interesting Literature, April 6, 2025, https://interestingliterature.com/2022/07/best-alexander-pope-quotes/.

Knowledge is a burning torch that enlightens, empowers, and differentiates. Knowledge at its essence is *"food of the soul."* However, knowledge can be dangerous and often very misleading and blinding if it is served or consumed in small amounts.

A little knowledge leads to the creation of false ideology in regard to different ethnic, racial, or religious groups. Seeds of this limited knowledge can be planted while we are **active or passive listeners.** Often, that knowledge is so strongly cemented in our minds that it leads to generalization and falsely placing people with similar ethnic, racial, or religious characteristics **in one already pre-made package ... stereotyping!**

It is that dangerous little knowledge that **poisons** our mentality without us often even being aware of it. It slowly conquers and impacts our views of ourselves and the people around us.

Knowledge changes us, for the better if the knowledge is researched and thorough. A little knowledge can create the mentality of **"us" vs. "them."** The result can be ethnocentrism, racism, sexism—all those "isms"! A little exposure or knowledge of differences can create the incorrect notion of possessing considerable knowledge, which can give one the false sense of being an expert. Negative learning can make us potential "victims" of self-created threats and/or allow scapegoating of people associated with certain genders, religions, races, or ethnicities.

At a point in our history, coeducation was argued to have negative impacts on the character and reproductive systems of females. Per Dr. Edward Clarke, Harvard University professor, "A woman's body can only handle a limited number of developmental tasks at one time. ... Girls who spend too much energy developing their minds during puberty could end up with undeveloped or diseased reproductive systems."[17]

---

[17] Edward Hammond Clarke, *Sex in Education: A Fair Chance for Girls* (S.l.: LECTOR HOUSE, 2024).

A Study of American Intelligence (1923) by Carl Brigham, professor at Princeton University, discusses the results of the U.S. Army Alpha Tests during World War I. Alpha Tests were given to army recruits to assess their intelligence levels. "The most mentally gifted recruits migrated to America from the 'most' intelligent European countries ... Germany, England, Scandinavia ... Italians, Jews, and Poles were labeled as mentally deficient."[18]

In the same *A Study of American Intelligence,* "American intelligence is declining and will proceed with an accelerated rate as racial admixture becomes more and more extensive."[19] The study contributed to the development of strict immigration laws in the 1920s.

Information comes to us from print, television, the internet, social media, radio, and daily one-to-one and group discussions ... a plethora of sources! The discerning reader will always evaluate the *source* and the *accuracy* of the information.

- *Exclusive vs. inclusive*
- *Quantity vs. quality*
- *Broad understanding vs. stereotypes*

What we consume matters!

- *Research what is said!* Do not just accept it because you heard it on a so-called "news" station.

- *Think for yourself!* Going with the flow might be easier and more convenient for you, but is it right, and are you being fair to others?

---

[18] Peter Sacks, *Tearing down the Gates Confronting the Class Divide in American Education* (Berkeley, CA: University of California Press, 2007).

[19] Wayne Au and Melissa Bollow Tempel, *Pencils down: Rethinking High-Stakes Testing and Accountability in Public Schools* (Milwaukee, WI: Rethinking Schools, 2012).

- ***Challenge yourself to grow*** in accurate knowledge of other people groups and individuals.
- ***Take ownership*** of that which affects you and those around you! Don't let misinformation be accepted as factual.

Some of the wisest quotes I have ever read are attributed to Rumi:

"Look for answers inside your questions."

"You are not a drop in the ocean. You are the entire ocean in a drop."

"As you start to walk on the way, the way appears."

Or as J. P. Morgan said, "Go as far as you can see. When you get there, you will be able to see farther."

#3: People do things for their reasons, not ours.

In any given situation, we each respond based on our own learning and socialization. A character on the Hallmark series *When Calls the Heart* declared, "These new people need to learn to follow the rules," to which his colleague responded, "They are called tourists, and they are good for the community." Having not watched anything but the ad for the episode, I don't know whether the rules were social or legal. I can only surmise that the "tourists" didn't know how things worked in that little frontier town.

An adult Latina student from southern Texas shared with our class that she was embarrassed when she was invited over for a barbecue and learned it was hamburgers on the grill. In her culture, a barbecue meant festival—complete with lavish, full-skirted dresses and a celebratory atmosphere. She later also shared that when Texas became part of the United States, her people became foreigners in their own land.

At the four-year public college where I was the Director of Financial Aid prior to coming to the community college, one of my staff came into my office very frustrated by a student. "I just don't trust him! He won't even look at me!"

When I inquired further, I learned that the young man was from one of our area Indian tribes. He had grown up learning that to drop his eyes to an older woman was a sign of respect. To the staff member, direct eye contact was a sign of honesty.

Another student declared, "911 is ruining our families!" What? What I learned was that her culture expected children to be well-behaved; discipline was a big part of that, though not physical or abusive in any way. Children had learned that if they didn't like the discipline they received, they called 911! Parents were now under a microscope and felt like they were losing control of their children.

I'm not sure where this really fits, but it is too significant to ignore. In the 1990s, during my time at the four-year public college, "political correctness" decisions were being made on a national level. Some terms obviously have a history that is denigrating and should be eliminated from our personal lexicons.

At the time, terms like African American, Native American, Hispanic American, and Asian American were labeled appropriate. During this time, Joann Sebastian Morris, who—as I remember—was the national head of the BIA (Bureau of Indian Affairs), visited our college.

Over lunch, I asked her why, if "Native American" was the correct term, the tribal colleges still called themselves Indian Community Colleges. Her answer resonates with me over 30 years later. "No one asked us."

She went on to explain that, in addition to "Indian" being the term of choice for her people, "Native American" had caused all manner of challenges because so many other people and people groups could claim to be Native American. The funding the tribes so desperately needed was bound up in confusing terminology.

I was pleased to see that the National Museum of the American Indian on the National Mall is not the Native American Museum. And I have yet to see an "African American Lives Matter" sign! "Black Lives Matter!"

Hispanic has largely been replaced by Latino/Latina/Latinx or the country of origin, followed by American. Asian American has also been mostly eliminated and replaced by the country of origin, followed by American. Other than for the grants needed, why must we even differentiate? Just "American" would be so much more inclusive and refreshing.

#4: No culture has a corner on all the good ideas.

Have you ever wondered what you are missing … what you don't know you don't know? As previously shared, some years ago, I took a group of high school and college students to the Navajo Reservation in northeast Arizona.

After a week of work, where our students were the teachers, we shared Sunday morning worship with our Navajo hosts. During worship, which was in Navajo but strangely understandable and meaningful, the little children were allowed to move around and play between the pulpit and the first row of the congregation. They were as quiet as church mice.

As I observed this unusual approach, I thought to myself, "Wow, we could learn something here! Children are not forced to sit in pews and act like little adults. They are allowed to be children … and maybe won't grow up disliking the concept of 'church'!"

It was also on that trip that I learned there was no word for "religion" in Navajo. In my interpretation, worship was about spiritual connection, not about denominational rituals or the rules of governance.

Indian cultures have historically believed that if you have more than you need, you have that which belongs to someone else. What a wise concept! When that happens or there is cause for celebration, tribal members often have, or had in years past, a giveaway.

While I was at the four-year public college, we had a partnership with some area tribes to provide education degrees for their students who could then go back to teach on the reservation. As so frequently happens when students are thrown into a complete cultural change, students often need periods to adjust.

Failing satisfactory academic progress for continued financial aid was not unheard of. As I would for any student, I considered the circumstances, helped develop an academic plan, and assisted a young woman from the Sioux Reservation to regain aid eligibility. When it came time for her to graduate, her grandmother was asked to give the prayer in her native tongue at graduation. I was invited to the graduation party afterward, thinking it would be a typical graduation party.

Instead, it was a giveaway. I was honored and shocked to receive a beautiful, handmade bone necklace and a star quilt, which I will cherish forever. Some years later, accepting such gifts as a financial aid director would have been against federal regulations, but I can't imagine the hurt and confusion I would have caused had I not been able to accept these gifts.

I just recently read in the college's alumni magazine that this same student is now deputy associate director of corrections with the U.S. Department of the Interior—Bureau of Indian Affairs Office of Justice Services. She has worked for 25 years with Indian Country inmates and jails throughout the United States. Imagine the loss had I not made the decision to grant an appeal.

Many cross-cultural trips with students to locations such as reservations, Appalachia, inner-island Jamaica, Uganda, the mountains of New Mexico, and Japantown in San Francisco were made with the goal of giving

… and we always came back having gained so much more than we ever could have given. Each location and culture had something to teach us.

What if we looked at each culture, religion, ethnicity—each individual—as though they had something to teach us, as though we needed to learn (not take!) something from that person to complete the puzzle? Try looking at work colleagues that way—from the company president to the janitor! We can learn from each one of them, regardless of their education or background.

We each need to overcome the belief that our approach is superior. Just because you are (or I am) the leader or the supervisor doesn't mean you (or I) have all the answers. We need others to get the job done. We hire others because of their expertise. Strong leaders and coaches will allow each person to contribute and do what they do best. As so well stated by Steve Jobs, "It doesn't make sense to hire smart people and then tell them what to do. We hire smart people so they can tell us what to do."[20]

Real life is no different! When Diversity, Equity, and Inclusion (DEI) became a focus for colleges and governmental bodies, the purposes and benefits were many. We learned more about one another.

When one of my staff members, who was on the first DEI Committee at our large community college, was hired by the Department of Education, he nominated me for the DEI position. He knew my passion for the topics and that we had the most diverse staff at the college. I hadn't thought about it! We recognized the benefits and learned from each other.

Reading Doris Kearns Goodwin's book *Team of Rivals* was extremely educational but, in some ways, very depressing. And I quote: "Lincoln

---

[20] "A Quote from Steve Jobs," Goodreads, accessed August 13, 2025, https://www.goodreads.com/quotes/8586131-it-doesn-t-make-sense-to-hire-smart-people-and-then.

had nothing but disdain for the discriminatory beliefs of the Know Nothings." In talking with his friend Joshua Speed, Lincoln continued, "Our progress in degeneracy appears to me to be pretty rapid. As a nation, we began by declaring that '*all men are created equal.*' We now practically read it, '*all men are created equal, except negroes.*' When the Know Nothings get control, it will read, '*all men are created equal except negroes, and foreigners, and catholics.*' When it comes to this, I should prefer emigrating to some country where they make no pretense of loving liberty—to Russia, for instance."[21]

When I read this, I felt the weight of current exclusionary movements within our country. Have we really made so little progress? All men are created equal, except many non-Caucasians, immigrants, and several religious groups, or you can fill in the blanks.

Consider the world as a giant classroom and learn from it! I greatly dislike the term "tolerance." Who wants to be tolerated? Not even just acceptance, though it is better than tolerance. *Embrace* diversity and learn from our differences. Together, we can prevent conflict and build a culture that is so much greater than the sum of its parts.

None of us has a corner on all the good ideas, no matter what our education, our culture, or our religion.

> "The truth was a mirror in the hands of God. It fell and
> broke into pieces. Everybody took a piece of it, and
> they looked at it and thought they had the truth."
>
> —Rumi

---

[21] Doris Kearns Goodwin and Richard Thomas, *Team of Rivals* (New York: Simon & Schuster, 2013) pgs. 180-181.

CHAPTER TWELVE

TOGETHER WE GROW

"Giving away money is an easy matter and in any man's power. But to decide to whom to give it and how large and when, and for what purpose and how, is neither in every man's power nor an easy matter. First, have a definite, clear, practical ideal—a goal, an objective."

—Aristotle

My life's work was my family, but I also had an extremely reward-ing work life. I was at various times a French teacher, a rep-resentative for Minnesota Woolens, a church choir director, an agent with Northwestern Mutual, a youth group director, a book editor, and a Director of Financial Aid for 34 years, having served at a four-year private, a four-year public, and two community colleges.

I reiterate that in 1987, I made an insurance call on the Dean of Students at a very small college and walked out as the Director of Financial Aid. I have yet to fully understand what happened there, but Financial Aid must have been my calling! Having to ask what a Direc-tor of Financial Aid does should have been a clue for the Dean, but he didn't flinch!

Financial aid seemed to combine everything I had done previously, from teaching to working with youth groups to financial planning.

"How do you find what fits? You don't. It finds you." (From a Hallmark movie—yes, I occasionally watch them!)

After four years at the first school, I was asked to apply for the open position at the neighboring four-year public college. During those years, I worked with our state association and EducationQuest Foundation, a Nebraska nonprofit whose mission is to help prepare students for college, on an elementary/middle school program called "Look to the Future." The curriculum fit into the regular curriculum—no set-aside time—and helped students focus on steps that would help them take appropriate coursework and develop skills needed in postsecondary education.

On several different days at the end of the year, we welcomed busloads of children from the reservations and other participating schools to observe chemistry experiments, experience math adventures, watch work on sculptures and paintings in the art studio, and enjoy lunch with the college president.

Typically, during lunch, the President would ask our guests what they might want to be when they grew up. Answers frequently heard from reservation students were casino workers or cowboys. It was what they knew, and is not unlike families like mine who have generations of teachers and administrators. Visiting a university campus and seeing that entire buildings, not just textbooks, were dedicated to math, science, or art was eye-opening for students. For some, their minds were opened and their perspectives changed. What a great program!

After six years at the four-year public college, I was asked to apply for the Financial Aid Director's position at the two-year community college in the town where we were living, saving a daily commute of 32 miles each direction and providing the opportunity to experience the value of community college.

In addition to serving as the Director of Financial Aid at the community college and teaching "Issues of Unity and Diversity" one evening a week, I started a multicultural club. It included many of our international students and met regularly and often in our home, and hosted a well-attended multicultural day each fall in an attempt to broaden the horizons of area high school students.

Among the keynote speakers were my next-door neighbor, who was a Muslim woman, our state's only black legislator, and a gay male student. Our club also created and hosted Martin Luther King Jr. Day events at the college and even presented the program for the junior high school in town.

Ten years later, after a perfunctory end to that experience that had nothing to do with the financial aid operation, I spent a year presenting financial aid workshops in high schools for EducationQuest. I was then hired as the Director of Financial Aid at Northern Virginia Community College (NOVA), the second largest community college in the country, miles away from anything I ever thought I would experience.

I had somehow—without design—gone from my first college, one of the smallest colleges in the country, to one of the largest. What seemed like an ending was just a new beginning. Though I never attended a community college, I found my mission in serving community college students. "The further you get from where you started, the closer you get to where you belong."

Living in northern Virginia and working at NOVA meant living in a microcosm of the world, and what the world will and should become. We had six full campuses and over 76,000 credit students at one point who came from 180 countries. I was living my United Nations dream, and every aspect of the "Issues of Unity and Diversity" course I developed and taught at the previous school.

Our incredible financial aid staff came from four or five continents at a given time and spoke 18 to 19 different languages. We were investigating and prosecuting fraud before most schools realized there was a problem. We hired well and focused on customer service and training—above and beyond rules and regs—to be the Best of the Best, and constantly utilized technology to work smarter, not harder.

Our staff regularly heard, "Can we automate that process?", "Don't paint yourself in a corner," "Document the heck out of it!", and "No headlines!" (One of my astute, and somewhat ornery, staff members hollered "No headlines!" to me as I was leaving the office one day for vacation!)

We learned about and from each other. I asked different staff members who had emigrated to share their stories of "Coming to America." Those experiences not only helped us better understand one another, but we also developed greater compassion for our students who were experiencing this strange new culture.

And we learned! No one culture has a corner on all the good ideas. "An individual's mind—once stretched by a new idea—can never return to its original size.... The goal is **synergy**—building a culture, an environment, that is so much greater than the sum of its parts" by valuing, embracing, and not fearing the differences.[22] We accomplished that as a staff.

Building Community

Assuming that people with common goals will just come together is incredibly optimistic and short-sighted. Building community within any organization must be intentional. NOVA Financial Aid needed to build community and then ensure a larger, compatible community through collaboration with other departments.

Though each member of any group or subset is ultimately responsible for the effectiveness of that group or subset, the leader of that group or subset must constantly monitor "community" and guide the group when the community is threatened.

[22] Stephen R. Covey, *The 7 Habits of Highly Effective People* (Blackstone Publishing, 2023).

When a sense of community begins to deteriorate in any organization, the lack of leadership and community can mean lost "customers," staff members, and revenue, and can ultimately destroy that organization.

Leading a business or organization is not an "honorary" position, and the selection of the leader should not be a popularity contest. Leadership is a responsibility and almost always involves work, which means that the leader must possess the necessary skill sets for the effectiveness and success of the organization.

CliftonStrengths assessments indicate that the 34 strengths are innate, but that in no way means a person is a born leader. Any one of those "talents" becomes a true strength only after knowledge and skill make it so. I do not profess to have all the answers. I am still learning and growing, and hope to do so as long as I live.

Throughout my working life, I have observed both very effective and very ineffective leaders. What I feel to be a frequent error in judgment is the leader who comes into an organization or business and immediately begins to make changes to put their own stamp on it without researching not only the "what" and "how" but also the "why" behind current practices.

- An individual new to an organization would be well advised to take time to evaluate what is working well and what might be improved or changed. Nothing destroys community more quickly than a leader who makes immediate changes without knowing what went into the current structure, which might have taken significant time, energy, and resources to build.

- Building community means listening first. Strong leaders will bring people together by sincerely caring about each member and valuing their ideas. Parsing out those ideas and being transparent in sharing the reasons for eventual decisions will help team members buy into the results.

- Sooner or later, every business or organization has conflict. Some conflicts are minor and dissipate on their own. Others must be addressed and resolved, or they grow into battles. Some individuals simply don't know how to exist without conflict in their lives and tend to keep the pot stirred. When an individual who thrives on conflict leaves the organization or business, whether by choice or not, even that vacant position can feel like an increase in staff.

- Leaders must recognize the difference between healthy and unhealthy competition within an organization. Healthy competition makes people better; unhealthy competition leads to conflict. Conflict resolution skills are a necessity for leaders.

- Leadership is, to me, the opposite of micromanagement. Leaders must provide the training and resources necessary for all team/staff members to do their jobs. Then, TRUST them to get the job done! Encourage each staff member to take ownership of their area of expertise and responsibility.

- Cross-train to the extent possible while minimizing duplication of effort, both so others understand the bigger picture and to ensure that the job can be done in the absence of the individual(s) with that primary responsibility.

- Bring staff together for productive purposes on a regular basis. Knowing other team members and sharing the big picture and individual responsibilities toward reaching business and organizational goals helps everyone feel part of the success and/or challenges of that community.

- Continually emphasize the mission and vision of the organization and ensure buy-in from all staff members. If buy-in wanes, find out why and work toward a solution.

- Create trusted partnerships with other areas of the organization or business that directly or indirectly impact your team's area of work. Working in silos is inefficient and can even lead to potentially illegal violations. Communicate with teams related to your responsibilities and work toward effective processes. More conflicts arise from a lack of knowledge or understanding of other departments than should ever happen. We are ALL on the bigger team!

- Take time to have fun together! We see a different side of our fellow workers in a relaxed setting. Including and encouraging everyone to participate in occasional, organized, purposeful activities, both inside and outside the office, helps build community more than just about anything. Be cognizant of and strive to avoid the traditionally busiest times of the year. When expense is a factor, consider everyone's financial limitations before planning outside activities. When anyone says we don't have time for that, reiterate the purpose. Everyone needs to relax and refresh. Taking time to do so is a must and can be healing for any organization.

Customer Service

When I arrived at NOVA, staff members were pretty burned out and not very trusting. Financial aid was understaffed, lacked the resources to address students' needs, and was getting pretty negative reviews across the college. A lot of work went into turning that around—a group effort, to be sure.

A few years later, other college departments wanted to emulate what we, as a team, had built and accomplished. With the help of two very supportive Executive Vice Presidents, we were able to totally revamp NOVA Financial Aid and add resources to provide greatly improved service for students and internal customers alike.

Campus financial aid staff were reporting to campus deans when I arrived, which caused inconsistencies and a lack of training and accountability. While still working closely with campus administrators, we were able to change the reporting structure to centralize it under the Director of Financial Aid, which allowed us to train, provide campus staff greater access to aid screens, and meet regularly with all individuals responsible for providing financial aid support to students.

When one Provost told me, some years into the new arrangement, that she had forgotten the Campus Financial Aid Manager didn't report to her, I knew it was working well. NOVA Financial Aid became a coordinated effort. Consistency and accountability increased exponentially. We were also able to hire Associate and Assistant Directors for new, critical positions: Information Technology, Campus Operations, Special Programs, Communications, File Review, Pell Grants and Loans, and Training.

The one existing Associate Director had responsibility for Return to Title IV Funds and managing the front staff. We were also able to add contractual services for a call center and another for self-help videos and a chatbot to address the thousands of unanswered calls Financial Aid students previously experienced. Adding verification assistance, loan letters, and default prevention initiatives, work-study and scholarship websites provided huge improvements for both students and staff.

For years, it has seemed to me that Financial Aid easily becomes a scapegoat when enrollment is down and rarely receives credit when enrollment is up! I recall that some years ago, an Admissions person even said, "Financial Aid didn't bring us enough students." Hmmm… Regardless, student service and customer service must be the mantra and an expectation for each and every person in any institution, business, or organization.

From my perspective, the tenets of customer service are these:

- Be proactive.
  - Anticipate what is needed.

- Provide clear messaging on websites, videos, and all communications.

- Set realistic expectations for external and internal customers.

- Provide timely updates for departments and outside organizations that also work with your same students/customers.

- Be knowledgeable.
  - Ensure all staff are trained, current, and on the same page.
  - Provide training for other departments that can assist customers with basic information.

- Be available.
  - Know when students/customers are most likely to contact or come into your offices (not always between 8 a.m. and 5 p.m.!).
  - If a phone number or live chat is offered, ensure lines are being answered (if necessary, publicize "blackout" times/dates).

- Be caring.
  - Yes, though the customer/student is NOT always right, it is ALWAYS about the customer/student!
  - Don't take customer/student frustration personally; it is NOT about you! (If it is, that's a different story!)
  - Just be nice! Everyone deserves kindness. Walk a mile in their moccasins!

- Be solution-oriented.
  - Define the problem.
  - No finger-pointing.

    ○ What will it take to fix the problem, and who should be involved?

    ○ How will the solution be communicated to ensure a response?

    ○ Empower the student/customer to the extent possible.

An early initiative at NOVA was mapping all the high schools and contacts within our service region, which was completed by the Associate Director for Communications. Previously, NOVA Financial Aid had offered financial aid workshops only to those high schools that were considered "feeder" schools.

Under the leadership of the Associate Director for Campus Operations and our Campus Managers, we began offering financial aid workshops for almost every high school in the region, which greatly increased exposure. We were offering information on financial aid, but families who might not have considered NOVA were able to ask questions and experience quality presentations by NOVA staff. Perhaps personal views of community college changed.

During my years at NOVA, the college grew by about 14,000 credit students, and financial aid recipients increased to three times the number of students receiving four times the financial assistance. We grew more each year than the total size of many small colleges! The total effort literally resulted in "Turning the Financial Aid Office Upside Down," the title of a session I provided with the assistance of different staff members at multiple conferences.

NOVA Financial Aid trained on financial aid issues and on a multitude of other pertinent topics—conflict resolution, ethics, diversity—to be the "best of the best." We had fun with psychogeometrics, a shape-based evaluation developed in 1978 by Dr. Susan Dellinger, Ph.D. Amazingly, that simple choice of a shape—circle, square, rectangle, triangle, or squiggly line—was almost always accurate in determining personality types. We might very well have all shapes within us, but some are dominant.

In a workshop of 215 NASFAA professionals, only five thought the results did not describe them. When I was first asked what shape I was, I said I felt like a circle with a box in it. I was told I had to pick one, but I soon realized that asking about the secondary shape of others revealed it had a significant influence on the first.

Our staff also provided full-day Financial Aid 101 training for nonfinancial aid staff, which created allies and prevented student bounce for basic financial aid questions. All financial aid staff members completed CliftonStrengths evaluations, and we focused on strengths at all meetings and within the office.

Staff members were encouraged to present, both internally and at conferences, which helped them build skills and gain confidence. Though monthly meetings sometimes were long, I felt it was important for associate and assistant directors to provide updates on their areas of responsibility. Through doing so, each became better at presenting, and all staff members knew what was happening across NOVA Financial Aid, had a better understanding of each area of responsibility, and realized the breadth and depth of our financial aid operation. We had to be "one"—no "them and us."

Our well-developed and regularly updated policies and procedures manual, which guided us, was managed by the Assistant Director of Training and was available online for all staff to reference and utilize as needed. We posted our CliftonStrengths charts in our kitchen area along with our mission and vision statements and core values, which I created with input from staff and which were reviewed/approved/embraced by all staff members.

Mission Statement

NOVA Financial Aid facilitates access to education for NOVA students by providing assistance in all areas of the financial aid process for the purpose of supporting student enrollment, retention, and program completion at Northern Virginia Community College.

Vision Statement

NOVA Financial Aid strives to balance access and accountability by providing responsible stewardship of all financial aid funds within a student-centered culture that works to eliminate financial barriers that would hinder student enrollment, retention, and program completion. NOVA Financial Aid is focused on becoming the best of the best among postsecondary institutions in all areas of the financial aid process.

Core Values

- Availability to students and the community
- Exemplary customer service
- Effective, consistent, and clear communication
- Appreciation for our incredibly rich diversity
- Integrity and irreproachable ethics
- Professionalism
- Staff development and training
- Mutual respect
- Continuous improvement
- Proactivity over reactivity
- A team approach that values each member
- Utilization of technology and all available resources to maximize outcomes

We took time to have fun, as well, celebrating within the office and spending a fall afternoon together annually, pre-COVID, outside the office. We floated the Potomac and laughed together during games/exercises on board the boat. We even went to an escape room one year—not my best personal endeavor.

Prior to holiday breaks, we had events such as a team gingerbread building contest, a white elephant gift exchange, and potlucks at various times. In any business, much less one as detailed and regulation-driven as financial aid, making time for fun together is critical in building a genuine, trusting, caring, and sincere culture and community—and in mitigating stress.

Together, we developed strong leaders. As Booker T. Washington stated, "Few things can help an individual more than to place responsibility on him (or her) and to let him know that you trust him." As stated by Oleg Vishnepolsky, "Nobody can be a leader if they do not trust their employees. No trust, no leadership—as simple as that."[23]

I did trust our NOVA staff to do their jobs! I had faith that our staff members were as committed to the work as I was. The fact that we regularly had clean audits and received high ratings on student/staff surveys reinforced that belief.

The first year I came to NOVA, student surveys for financial aid were abysmal! Within a few years, we consistently were among the highest ratings. When COVID caused offices to close and work to be done remotely, NOVA Financial Aid didn't miss a beat. The work of the College Financial Aid Office continued as it had before.

Our campus staff met with students through private Zoom meeting rooms to assist them just as they had been doing face-to-face. A

---

[23] "Oleg Vishnepolsky - Daily Mail - Mailonline," LinkedIn, accessed August 13, 2025, https://www.linkedin.com/in/vishnepolsky/?original_referer=https%3A%2F%2Fwww.google.com%2F.

personal lesson I learned during COVID was that I needed to get up every day and prepare for a workday just as I would when going to the office. When I looked better, I felt better! (I also learned that I had better results if I put on my eye make-up *before* I had two cups of coffee!)

I do remember asking at one point if I could come back to the office two days a week, although college offices were closed. I really needed that change of location, dual screens, and access to my office, which was approved.

Since COVID, much debate and deliberation have ensued over hybrid or remote work versus all staff being back in the office. My contention is that the individuals who don't get the job done when working remotely are the same ones who didn't get it done when in the office! Though I heartily agree that building a strong team requires regular face-to-face communication and teamwork, requiring everyone to be back in the office on a daily basis could be counterproductive.

Moreover, some administrators are so paranoid about flexible hours that they require all staff to be in the office during the exact same times every day. Especially in high population areas like DC and northern Virginia, adding more cars to the highways during the heaviest traffic times of the day means staff members are on the road for more hours each day.

When I quit commuting 32 miles one way to the public four-year institution where I worked in Nebraska, a much lighter traffic area, I made the comment, "I hadn't realized how heavy the baggage was until I put it down." I got the equivalent of a day of my life back each week!

Staff members who are not receiving the larger salaries could also find more affordable housing outside the areas closest to NOVA campuses. Finding more affordable housing requires longer commutes, and for many young families, higher childcare expenses and time away from their families. Allowing flexible but regular hours and/or remote or hybrid work lessens the pain of many of these issues. If staff members are not responsible for getting the job done, a different conversation is necessary.

I have come to believe that leaders who require all workers to return to the office are oblivious to the added burdens on staff and/or the potential effectiveness of remote workers. Some seem more concerned about building owners who aren't making as much money from rental contracts than they are about staff members. Those rental contracts also greatly expand the footprint and expense of the institution, which must then be passed on to students! Let's rethink this!

I have always felt that one of my responsibilities as the Director was to help staff members get to where they wanted to be. Encouraging staff members to develop their skills and reach new goals often means losing wonderful talent and starting over with training a new hire, but nothing is more rewarding than helping staff members grow and advance in their careers.

As I was planning for retirement, one staff member left to work for the Department of Education and two were hired by NASFAA, our national financial aid association. Another was hired by Maryland Judicial to manage their training. Other staff members have been promoted, both within NOVA and when hired by outside entities.

After I retired, some financial aid staff were hired away from Financial Aid by Admissions. Had these truly been advancements, so be it, but these lateral moves were because Admissions positions paid more. Staff members needed a salary increase, but paying more for Admissions staff was demeaning to financial aid staff, who needed most of the same skills plus a great deal of detailed financial aid information. Regardless, as hard as it is to say goodbye to valued staff members, the joy of watching them advance is worth it ... and the process of building strong staff members begins anew.

Train, communicate what needs to be done, and then get out of the way—trust staff to do their jobs. Listening to staff members is vital. Hearing them is even more so!

I regularly told our NOVA staff that I would put them up against any financial aid staff in the country. I'm not sure they always believed me, but I was absolutely serious. They were that good! I didn't think about it at the time, but a quote credited to Tom Peters, business management expert, in 2014 says it well: "Leaders don't create followers, they create more leaders." Stated even more strongly by Simon Sinek, "The greatest contribution of a leader is to make other leaders."

NOVA Financial Aid staff members included many leaders and emerging leaders. The talent was there; providing opportunities for skill-building and continuous growth in knowledge helped build talent into strength.

CHAPTER THIRTEEN

PROFESSIONAL OPPORTUNITIES

Working within our state, regional, and national associations, both in Nebraska and in Virginia, presented opportunities I could never have imagined. Within three to four years of entering the profession, I was elected to office in NEASFAA, the Nebraska Association of Student Financial Aid Administrators. Serving as President at the state level led to my involvement in numerous committees at the regional level, including co-chairing the regional conference, and later becoming President for RMASFAA, the eight-state Rocky Mountain Association of Student Financial Aid Administrators.

Twice, I co-presented sessions in beautiful locations for each of the eight state conferences within our region, once on Conflict Management and once on Diversity. Traveling with my young, black colleague from Kansas for one of the series some 25 years ago was another lesson in prejudice. Small towns in mid-America had little exposure to diversity. Some still don't.

When driving to our Wyoming destination, my colleague and I took a side trip to visit a cemetery on the Wind River Reservation, shared by the Eastern Shoshone and Northern Arapaho tribes. Sacajawea is buried there, with her infant son on one side and an adult son on the other. A revered chief is also buried in that same area.

We were at the cemetery right before Memorial Day, and the people were out raking the graves and placing stones around the edges and flowers on the graves. The site was remote, spiritual, and so peaceful. I've noticed through the years that military veterans are honored and highly esteemed members of each tribe.

Death is intrinsically part of life. Whether due to my family history, my interest in history in general, or in cultural commonalities and differences, life experiences have included stops at many cemeteries and historic locations, some of which defy understanding.

Walking among the old stones at the top of the hill in Harper's Ferry or among the above-ground tombs due to high water levels in New Orleans is peaceful for me. Seeing rows and rows of crosses covered by colorful flowers at a Mexican cemetery on Dia de los Muertos feels celebratory. Attending a memorial service for the husband of a PEO sister at Arlington National Cemetery, where I have gone many times, was emotional.

Assuming there was one service for all and inadvertently attending Memorial Day services at the confederate cemetery in Manassas was a learning experience. We were met by women dressed as southern belles, and I was asked if I wanted to join the Daughters of the Confederacy; there were still 12 active chapters. A second service was held later across the road at the Union Cemetery.

Walking the grounds at Harper's Ferry, Gettysburg, Fredericksburg, Bull Run, Antietam, the Battle of Little Big Horn, Wounded Knee, Dachau Concentration Camp in Germany, the 9/11 Memorial in NYC, the Oklahoma City National Memorial, and standing above the USS Arizona at Pearl Harbor were somber but extremely impactful lessons in life and death—and reminders of humankind's heart-wrenching inability to solve problems without violence. When will we ever learn?

I have walked the monuments on the National Mall many times. Some, like the FDR, Lincoln, Jefferson, Washington, and MLK Jr., honor but also educate. Some of the monuments seem in some respect to glorify war. The war memorial that seems most real is the Korean Monument at night. When the dim lights shine up from the ground and show the somber expressions and heavy packs of soldiers in the field, I can almost feel the pain of war.

When my brother and sister-in-law visited me in Virginia and we walked the Mall, my brother used the directory at the monument and found the names of seven friends on the Vietnam Veterans Memorial wall. One was a classmate and the son of our high school English and French teacher.

On more than one occasion, I have been at Washington airports when honor flights arrived, which were originally for WWII veterans only. Before they began including Korean and Vietnam veterans, I was waiting for my flight at the airport when I noticed that a whole group of those deplaning were wearing Vietnam Veteran caps. At one point in history, Vietnam veterans were demonized for taking part in that conflict, though the vast majority certainly didn't volunteer for the job. Knowing that, I instinctively began clapping—and was deeply moved when the rest of the concourse joined in the applause.

At one time, when I was RMASFAA President, a conflict developed when the regional tribal college conference was held at the same time as the RMASFAA Conference. We met to discuss it, and by adjusting dates, came to a decision that would allow members to attend both.

A colleague from Colorado College met me at the airport in Denver, and with a colleague from the American Indian Foundation, both of whom were former RMASFAA Presidents, attended the blessing of the Foundation's new offices in Denver. The ceremony and blessing with sage and smoke were truly spiritual and beautiful.

The Big Denver Powwow, a gathering of tribes from across the country, was being held at the same time. My RMASFAA colleagues, John and Jim, and I went to the Powwow. We were seated in the stands watching the dancing when John asked if I knew who one of the dancers was. I recognized her immediately as Marilyn, the administrative assistant on the television show *Northern Exposure*, which I never missed. John knew her and asked if we wanted to meet her, which of course we did. We walked out on the floor and met Marilyn, played by Elaine Miles, and her mother. Their dress and headdress were reflective of northwest tribes, with the headdress looking somewhat like a fish basket. I loved the dancing and was thrilled to meet Marilyn.

At the national level, I was privileged to serve on the NASFAA Board of Directors and multiple committees, including an early multicultural concerns committee, with amazing colleagues from across the country. For several years, we annually crafted a Carnival of Learning that encouraged low-income elementary school students in the area of our conference to consider and plan for college. The Carnivals were held the day before each NASFAA conference in more beautiful locations.

I also chaired the NASFAA Leadership Development and Professional Advancement Committee and Conference for one year. My closing remarks were rather emotional; I'm not sure if that was the result of exhaustion that quickly turned into sickness or the incredible participation of attendees.

After moving to Virginia, I chaired the VASFAA Conference, served as VASFAA President, and chaired the Southern Association of Student Financial Aid Administrators (SASFAA) Conference in 2020. When the title of the conference, "Courage, Compassion, Collegiality: A Survivor's Guide for Uncharted Waters," was chosen over a year before, we had no idea how appropriate it was—and continues to be. One month after the conference, the COVID national emergency was declared. We were fortunate, after over a year of planning, to even be able to hold that conference.

I presented many times at all levels of the profession, for the State Department, the National Indian Education Conference, staffers on the Hill, the Advisory Committee, and the House Committee on Education and the Workforce, and served on the Program Integrity Negotiated Rulemaking Committee, which addressed a plethora of regulations.

Return to Title IV, the requirement to calculate the potential return of a portion of the federal aid received by the student when a student withdraws or quits attending before the end of the term of the award, was the one issue among the many we were negotiating that was not given the time needed. After many years, the inequity of that rule was finally addressed, but it is still being reevaluated to this day.

I was asked by the Association of Community College Trustees (ACCT) to serve on the Student Loan Negotiated Rulemaking Committee, as well. I was placed on the committee at the initial meeting and left the room with another Financial Aid Director to decide who would chair the committee.

When I came back, an attorney from a proprietary school had convinced the group that he should be on the committee instead of me, a second community college representative. I was told later that he never appeared for any of the negotiated rulemaking sessions. Oh well … I guess he thought the position was honorary.

During the process of securing assistance for military men and women impacted by 9/11 and the ensuing military activity, I was asked to participate in roundtable discussions with Dupont Circle organizations in D.C. that helped develop Post 9/11 VA benefits.

Post 9/11 benefits were invaluable for military men and women, but a number of men and women who took classes had physical and mental challenges from trauma that should have been addressed first. Colleges and universities were charged with providing post-traumatic stress disorder (PTSD) interventions without having the training to do so.

I recall standing at an information session chaired by Bob Shireman and saying, "Colleges and universities want to help, but the VA has, in essence, given colleges an unfunded mandate to do so without providing us the resources we need." The implementation of 9/11 aid provided much-needed assistance but was a bit rocky, to say the least.

I attended a conference sponsored by the National Defense Industrial Association at which Elizabeth Dole and many wounded warriors spoke. To see and hear men and women with such catastrophic physical and mental injuries was heartbreaking. A second meeting hosted by Wounded Warriors further emphasized the challenges. "War is Hell!" (General William Tecumseh Sherman). "When will we ever learn?" (Pete Seeger).

So many incredible memories! Each one was a growth opportunity for me. President Obama was on our campus twice. Once, I was seated about 15 feet from him as he presented. Another time, he came to the campus theater in Alexandria to sign the bill that eliminated the Federal Family Education Loan program (FFELP). The Executive VP to whom I reported was surprised when one of the higher Department of Education officials gave me a big hug that day. I knew him from post 9/11 and other meetings. I think my credibility went up.

As I arrived at the Capitol for one of the sessions where I was asked to train Hill staffers on financial aid, we learned that a black unit from Carolina would that afternoon be receiving Congressional Medals of Honor for their omitted and forgotten heroic contributions during WWII.

As we ended the training, I ran to the Rotunda and stood at the rail in the balcony to watch the ceremony. Many of the remaining recipients were in wheelchairs, but most awards were presented posthumously to family members. Tears, tears, and more tears for those who had waited so long to be recognized and for the bittersweet honors accepted by family members for those who didn't live to experience this day.

On another occasion, our NASFAA President and CEO, Justin Draeger, invited me to meet with Rep. Virginia Foxx, Chair of the House Education and the Workforce Committee, or whatever the name was then. The group included an aid administrator from a proprietary school, a staff member or two, Dr. Foxx, Justin, and me. We had a worthwhile conversation on the needs of our schools.

As we were breaking, Dr. Foxx and I started discussing our backgrounds in education and how we got to this point. She really laughed when I told her I had originally been a French teacher and had just moved from one foreign language to another. In more recent years, Dr. Foxx has seemed like a different person. All things "education" have become so politicized.

I have long been a huge supporter of undocumented individuals who have been in this country since childhood. These individuals and those without legal papers are now at great risk under the new administration.

My first encounter with the topic was early in my career when a young woman came into my office in tears. She had been living in the country with her grandmother since she was a toddler and didn't know she was undocumented. As she was graduating from high school, she told her grandmother she had decided to go to college. Her grandmother said she couldn't; they couldn't afford it. The student insisted that she had good grades and had learned at school that she could apply for scholarships and other financial aid. After her grandmother insisted that she could not go, she was finally told by her grandmother that she couldn't apply for financial aid because she was undocumented.

In April 2001, Senator Orrin Hatch, a Republican from Utah, and Senator Dick Durbin, a Democrat from Illinois, sponsored Senate Bill S.1291, which became known as the DREAM Act. The bill was supported by over 50% of senators from both sides of the aisle.

Whether directly responsible for the change of support or not, 9/11 happened a few short months later. The DREAM Act never passed and has since been viewed contentiously. To this day, I believe the DREAM Act would support the "greater good." When it takes so many years for an individual to receive a green card, we need to rethink the laws and the processes. Our country was built on immigration. Without immigration, some states would have a negative population growth and workforce. In addition, we need a more effective worker program.

I did a lot of research and wrote an article on the DREAM Act for *The Financial Aid Transcript*, which then became a presentation at a NASFAA Conference in Seattle with my financial aid colleague from California, Paul Phillips.

That presentation, and my regional visit as a NASFAA Board member to the Western Association of Financial Aid Administrators (WASFAA) Conference in Anchorage, ultimately led to my going twice to Uganda with Paul and his wife Jean to work with the Aids Orphans Education Trust (AOET). I haven't believed in coincidences for many years. Things happen for a reason. Always be open to opportunities.

After the WASFAA Conference in Anchorage, which included dancing by Tlingit tribal members, Paul, our NASFAA Chair and his wife, another aid administrator from New York, and I toured a bit of Alaska. Paul was in charge of site selection for WASFAA events, and several stops were for that purpose. Other stops included the site where the Iditarod starts, a whale watch on the bay, a visit to Alyeska Ski Resort, and visiting an Eklutna Indian village. I was taken by the mixture of cultures so evident there.

The Eklutna had been proselytized by the Russian Orthodox Church. An older, small church with an "onion-shaped" steeple on top sat behind a newer, larger church with a similar but larger steeple. What was really fascinating was the cemetery in the back. Each grave had a little house that looked much like a dollhouse built over the top of the grave. We were told that these spirit houses were where the spirit lived when the body died.

Another wonderful opportunity unexpectedly presented itself when the Director/VP from Northern Virginia Community College's office of international students/studies asked me if I could go to Pretoria, South Africa, to represent NOVA at the Education USA Conference in 2010. He knew I had already traveled to Africa and likely had the necessary paperwork and requirements to go. The conference was for Education USA representatives from all the Sub-Saharan embassies and college representatives from the U.S.

I jumped at the opportunity! I took a few days of vacation on the front and back ends of the conference to see as much as possible. After a perfectly enjoyable flight of 22 hours, seated next to a South African man who had taught Rory Sabatini (math, not golf!) and that landed only momentarily in Senegal, I arrived in Johannesburg, most frequently called J-Burg.

From Johannesburg, I flew to Cape Town, arriving after dark. As I was riding in the van from the airport to my hotel, I began visiting with an older couple who were just returning from the Netherlands. I asked about tours and shared that I wasn't able to book everything I wanted to see within the limited time I had in Cape Town. At first, they commiserated, but then said that they had a friend who was just starting out as a tour guide. They told me, "If you call him, he will likely be able to pick you up at your hotel and take you wherever you want to go."

Though I would advise my children and grandchildren to NEVER do such a thing, I called the number they provided. Bright and early the next morning, I was picked up by a very nice young man of Indian descent.

As we drove down the coast, I was surprised by the palm trees and tropical feel. When we got to the tip of the continent, the ocean breezes were crisp, and the mileage signs to points around the globe were a reminder of the breadth of this world.

Driving back up the east side, we stopped at a wild penguin colony, had lunch along the ocean where a great white shark had been spotted, and toured a winery or two in Stellenbosch.

My guide's phone rang, and I was invited to dinner at their home by his girlfriend. I learned she was of English descent, and her son had just graduated from Oxford and was in graduate studies at Harvard. They were really hoping to do a home exchange for a few weeks so they could visit the U.S., but had no idea how far northern Virginia was from Harvard! Nonetheless, we had a lovely meal and great conversation at their home high on a bluff overlooking the ocean, after which I was driven back to my hotel. What an incredible day!

After another day or two of formal tours, I flew back to Johannesburg and then traveled to Pretoria for the conference. I met so many wonderful people, one of whom sent her children to Northern Virginia Community College. I still hear from her on occasion.

One noon, I was able to meet a former student and member of our Multicultural Club from Nebraska for lunch. She lived about 15 minutes from where I was staying! Other U.S. colleges attended the conference. More than one highly respected university wanted to partner with NOVA. Our sheer numbers would have added transfer students to their totals. At that time, we transferred more students annually to George Mason University than they took in each year as freshmen.

The conference was amazing and included a trip to the Cradle of Humankind, where we viewed the remains of "Little Foot," a nearly complete skeleton, still largely encased in rock, dating back 2.5 million years. Another tour took us through the area with a guide, who stopped at one of the "apartheid" settlements where hundreds of people lived in makeshift shacks. The area looked much like the refugee camp in Uganda.

We were invited inside one of the corrugated metal "homes," which gave us a pretty clear picture that the end of apartheid had not changed much for the black population of South Africa. Education had not been offered to blacks, which created a huge population without the knowledge and skills to support themselves effectively. It feels like we are repeating that mistake by not addressing education for undocumented students in the U.S.

We also went to a school in Soweto where protests resulted in killings, including that of Hector Peterson, and we toured the home of Nelson and Winnie Mandela. The last day of the conference was a celebration, complete with a banquet and traditional dancing by our African counterparts.

The conference was followed by an optional safari north of Pretoria but not as far as Kruger, which, of course, I took. We stayed in a safari lodge and traveled in an open-sided game viewing vehicle. In addition to a raft of other beautiful animals, I remember seeing many zebras, rhinos, and giraffes in South Africa that I had not seen in Uganda.

I drove on most of my trips back and forth from Virginia to Iowa. On one occasion when I flew to or from D.C., I struck up a conversation with my seatmate, who turned out to be White House Executive Pastry Chef Roland Mesnier. We talked a great deal. He told me his story and that he had written a cookbook. I told him I would love to buy one for my husband, who had never met a carbohydrate he didn't like!

Chef Mesnier and his wife invited me to their home in a wooded area not far from Fairfax and Centreville. He autographed several books for me. Roland and Mrs. Mesnier were both so warm, gracious, and trusting of someone they didn't know at all. Chef Mesnier served through several administrations. Apparently, good food transcends politics.

On multiple occasions with different family members, we have spent Christmas Eve in Santa Fe, shopping from the artisans under the awning of the Palace of Governors and attending Christmas Eve services at the Cathedral Basilica of St. Francis of Assisi.

Santa Fe closes down Canyon Road on Christmas Eve, and people stroll the long street, singing Christmas carols, enjoying beverages, warming by little farolitos, and admiring the hundreds of luminarias that line sidewalks and rooftops. For two years in a row, after purchasing bracelets from a silversmith under the awning at the Palace of Governors, we were invited to Santo Domingo Pueblo for dancing on Christmas morning, which begins at sunrise.

The second year, we had our granddaughter with us and attended the dancing on our way to Phoenix. I couldn't identify the man who invited us since he was one of the kachina dancers who represent deified ancestral spirits of the Pueblo people in ceremonial dances. Another experience to remember that we could have missed. We were invited and welcomed, but we were the only Caucasians there.

Santa Fe, New Mexico, has always been a favorite location. While serving on the NASFAA board and again while part of a national group of administrators sponsored by the Bill and Melinda Gates Foundation to explore emergency aid for college students, we stayed at Hotel Santa Fe, a beautiful and peaceful hotel owned by the Picuris Pueblo tribe. I recently stayed there again on two different occasions on my way home from Arizona.

Before meetings started for the Board and again before meetings on emergency aid, I took NASFAA Board members and, the second time, a staff member who was part of the emergency aid group to Bandelier National Monument. I remember well the doubtful looks I got when mentioning that the opening at the center of the kiva floor was called the sipapu—until the guide repeated that bit of knowledge. Group members climbed the log ladders and enjoyed exploring the cliff dwellings. My staff member is a rather tall individual and still laughs about almost getting stuck on his climb.

The only other tribally owned hotel where we have stayed was on the Pima-Maricopa Reservation in Chandler, where our son-in-law was working as a manager with Marriott. Indian flute music and gorgeous paintings welcomed us as we entered, the restaurant was 5-star, the pools refreshing, and the room spacious. We even rode the peaceful adjoining land via horseback for several hours to see the wild horse herds, including a new crop of foals.

I asked if the concierge would share the history with me, and our son-in-law arranged it. I learned that Caucasians traveling to the gold fields had come back through the Pima-Maricopa Reservation and set up farming decades before, using all the water for irrigation and shutting off access for the tribes. After almost 100 years, the tribes had just gotten water back in the early 2000s, and a beautiful and very welcome river now runs through the reservation and hotel property.

When traveling cross-country by car, I try to stop and enjoy at least one or two points of interest along the way. One such trip included the day I spent at the Kentucky Horse Park, a stunning 1200-acre farm near Lexington where Kentucky Derby winners were pastured, and graves and statues of champions like Man o'War, Secretariat, and John Henry are memorialized.

On another trip, I purposely drove to Carlisle, Pennsylvania, so I could try to tour the Carlisle Indian School. I said "try" because the school is on an army base, and clearance is required. My background check was amazingly quick, and I walked the grounds, which I pretty much had to myself.

General Pratt was the one who executed the concept of removing Indian children from their families to "take the Indian out of the child and save the man." Children were disciplined for speaking their own languages or displaying any part of their cultures. Jim Thorpe, Olympic champion, was one of the thousands of children "educated" at Carlisle. Some of the buildings had notations indicating that they were built by students.

The most devastating part of the day was walking through the cemetery. To the extent that children were identified when the cemetery was moved, headstones displayed names, ages, and tribes of children from all over the country. I couldn't help thinking of dying children and wondering if the children had anyone to comfort them, or if the parents even knew their children had died. At the school in Genoa, Nebraska, I am told the cemetery has not yet been located.

"There are two moments in life—those you miss and those you seize." Early in my travels for industry meetings, I began taking a few vacation days around each meeting to see the area. Missing conference sessions to do so would not be the sign of a good leader. Taking a few vacation days on either side of meetings is not that expensive when transportation to the area is part of the meeting expense. You've already spent a fair amount of time and money getting there, so make the most of it!

Travel is very educational, especially if well-focused. I personally love historic points of interest. Even short explorations pointed me to places where I wanted to return. And after a busy and intense conference, a little R&R is always appreciated.

After an RMASFAA board meeting, a dear friend and colleague took a small group to Yellowstone National Park, an area she knew extremely well. She and I were in the gift shop at one of the geyser basins when a woman came running into the shop crying that her husband had just been knocked off the path by a bull elk.

Instead of going to our car, as common sense might dictate, we went out to see what had happened! The cow herd of a bull elk in the rut had become separated by the path that led out into the basin. Another bull elk was bugling close by, and the bull with the herd was going crazy. He had wandered about 50 yards away by the time we went out, but gradually worked his way back.

That big guy then charged the path about 15 feet from where we were standing! After dislodging his antlers from the rail, he eventually gathered his herd together and settled down a little. The other bull retreated.

That experience and another watching the elk around one of the hotels were exercises in a complex social phenomenon. Incredible!

My friend then took us to a spot on the Yellowstone River where we enjoyed "hotpotting." Very hot springs flow into the edge of the river. When mixed with the cold water of the Yellowstone in small rocked-in areas, the water felt like a wonderful hot tub. It pays to have someone in the know act as a guide!

When NASFAA was in Boston a few years ago, I took time to visit my last five states. I rented a car and drove by myself west from Boston, south through Connecticut, east across Rhode Island, back into Massachusetts, took the ferry across to Nantucket, drove north to Plymouth Rock, and on to Portsmouth, New Hampshire, and up the coast of Maine. Since that first trip, I have gone back to the area twice—once with our daughters and friends and once with my sister-in-law, who has been my traveling companion on many trips.

On that first trip, I stopped at every beach and lighthouse in Maine and ate lobster that was better and less expensive than I could ever have imagined. Strawberry Banke in Portsmouth is a wonderful historic area where I unexpectedly found information about Admiral Farragut, the namesake of my hometown in Iowa, whom I associated with Mobile Bay in Alabama, but not New Hampshire!

I never knew how a spot in the middle of Iowa was named after Admiral Farragut until my sister was researching for a CCC museum in her community in northern Iowa. She learned from research completed for Farragut's centennial that the man who donated land for my hometown and the local cemetery several generations ago had been in the navy and had admired Admiral Farragut.

Before that find, we laughingly always said Admiral Farragut had sailed down the Nishnabotna River outside our little berg. Since sandbars are visible in the river much of the year, that was highly unlikely.

In spring 2022, I was honored with a lifetime membership in VASFAA and with a SASFAA Certificate of Appreciation for Extraordinary Service and Dedication to the Profession. I was humbled and honored to receive the Allen W. Purdy Distinguished Service Award, one of the highest awards given by our national association, at NASFAA Conference 2022.

Our son, Shawn, and daughter-in-law, Tina, were there to support me. Tina asked me if I was nervous before my acceptance presentation. Unlike the shaking knees after my high school solo, I was not. Numerous presentations—and, of course, preparation—do make a difference!

We took a day after and traveled the hill country of Texas, visiting historic Gruene, dining at the restaurant in the old mill, hitting a few wineries along the way, and even stopping in Luckenbach. I had no idea it was so small, but it becomes huge for musical events! What a memorable day!

CHAPTER FOURTEEN

EXPANDED EXCERPTS FROM NASFAA PURDY AWARD ACCEPTANCE SPEECH ... FORGIVE THE REPETITION!

As you know by now, while in Nebraska, I volunteered as a facilitator for experiential Alternatives to Violence (AVP) workshops in the prison system and, on two different trips, facilitated three workshops in northern Uganda where the Lord's Resistance Army was still terrorizing the villages.

Alternatives to Violence focuses on Transforming Power and the following precepts: Respect for Self, Caring for Others, Expect the Best, Think Before Reacting, and Ask for a Nonviolent Solution. And, I would add, Always Consider the Other's Viewpoint. The precepts apply anywhere! I used many of the exercises with our financial aid staff.

I come from many generations of educators and believe that education is/*can be* the great equalizer—*if* it is offered with quality instruction and resources to *all* students at all levels, regardless of socioeconomic status.

I strongly support Pell Grants and education for inmates. What logic is there in throwing anyone in prison with no training offered while they are there—and expecting them to come out better for the experience?

In the early 1990s, legislators determined that providing money for convicted felons to attend school was unfair to those on the outside who didn't qualify. In their eyes, that money was not well spent. I wonder if those same legislators ever considered the cost of housing inmates, especially when recidivism comes into play and individuals are incarcerated on more than one occasion. Does it not make more sense to provide education and skills for inmates so they can earn a living legally when they are paroled or have served their time?

College courses alone might not be enough. Combining education with Alternatives to Violence workshops, CliftonStrengths evaluations—so inmates know they HAVE strengths and how to work within them for a better life—and a work-release program prior to release, which, by the way, was recommended by the inmates with whom I worked, would further enhance the success rate, reduce recidivism, and help inmates re-enter society with hope and training for something better. The combination would be *powerful*!

My dad's charge was "Make the world a better place for your having been here." As a lifelong educator and administrator, Dad was also a huge supporter of the public school system.

I can no longer ask my father for his opinion, but I firmly believe that he would agree that using public funds for school vouchers is a mistake. Not only are private—and even charter—schools largely unregulated, but they aren't required to accept all students. Those students with high academic, athletic, and other talents will be accepted, along with those whose parents can afford the tuition above voucher amounts. Public schools will get the rest. Once again, the "haves" are advantaged, and public schools and public-school teachers will lose funding and support.

Club sports result in similar inequities. The pendulum swings once again. If public schools are slipping, let's figure out how to fix the problems—not abandon one of the greatest assets of this country.

I remember the inequities faced by students in some states before federal policy created standards for the entire country. And now, we have an administration that wants to hand education requirements back to the states—more opportunities for inequities. How many years will pass before we realize the mistakes we are currently making—or remaking—as a country?

William James said, "The greatest use of life is to spend it on something that will outlast it." Or as my Yogi tea "fortune" told me, "Let your need be to help those in need." As financial aid administrators and educators, *I felt we did that every day!*

With current efforts to dismantle the Department of Education and to make states responsible for education—and presumably aid administration—the profession is a bit in limbo. Aid administration could look much different in the coming months. It will be "interesting." ("Interesting" is my new favorite word to describe anything that seems a bit inexplicable or even wacky.)

Whether or not the administration of financial aid becomes a career that no longer mirrors the service-focused career of years gone by, we must maintain the focus on the greater good. When you have a worthwhile career in any area, act as if what you do makes a difference because it does!

But we each can and must do more. Get outside your comfort zone until you are comfortable being uncomfortable. Choose to do the right thing! Have high expectations for yourself, your family, your students, and your staff. Don't buy into this "them vs. us" attitude—or one day you will find that "them" is us! If we set expectations high, people will meet them. If we set them low, they will meet them. We must aim *above* the mark to hit the mark.

I realized pretty early that "making the world a better place for my having been here" is not a one-time event. If it isn't continuous, progress deteriorates, and we move backward. Please know that I don't pretend to be able to individually change the world.

An inspiration to me is the story of the little boy on the beach with his grandfather. Many starfish washed up on shore overnight. The little boy kept picking them up and throwing them back into the ocean. His grandfather said, "Let's go home. There are too many … it just won't matter." As he kept throwing starfish into the ocean, the little boy said, "It will to this one—and this one."

I don't pretend to be a leadership expert. I have had successes but also disappointments—some totally unexpected. I can count the serious disappointments in single digits and have tried to look in the mirror to determine what I might have changed. Some were about power and control, and I was not the "top dog."

It is impossible to negotiate with someone who insists on defeating you, especially when power is in the other court. Regardless, all are learning opportunities. "Never let success get to your head—nor defeat get to your heart" (anonymous).

I also strongly believe in karma and have never felt the need to "get even." If I did, I would be part of the problem. As the Dalai Lama said, "Remember that not getting what you want is sometimes a wonderful stroke of luck!" Be careful what you wish for, you just might get it!

I have also come to believe over the decades that there is no such thing as a coincidence. Things happen for a reason. Some of my greatest disappointments have allowed and encouraged incredible opportunities that I couldn't imagine being absent from my life!

Though I am not a high-risk taker, I agree with Wayne Gretzky, "You miss 100% of the shots you don't take." Do your homework first, but don't avoid failure at all costs. We often learn more from failures than we do from successes.

"God grant me the serenity to accept the things I cannot change, courage to change the things I can, and the wisdom to know the difference" (The Serenity Prayer). I also tend to believe what was so eloquently stated by Eleanor Roosevelt: "No one can make you feel inferior without your permission." Don't allow anyone to make you feel "less than."

CHAPTER FIFTEEN

INGREDIENTS FOR LEADERSHIP

"She believed she could, so she did."

—Roald Dahl, *Matilda*

A recent gift and subsequent read is Gandhi's autobiography, *The Story of My Experiments with the Truth*. Reading works by such impactful leaders is not just a wonderful pastime but another opportunity to learn and grow. Gandhi epitomizes servant leadership.

Even before starting this book, I believed that leadership should be about others and not be self-serving, but the reality is that we reap what we sow. "You can't help someone else uphill without getting closer to the top yourself."

When I was Director of Financial Aid at my first community college, I was told that one of the longtime high school guidance counselors in our area said that I was "tough but fair." At the time, I was a bit taken aback; I interpreted "tough" as somewhat negative and not who I thought I was.

In hindsight, sometimes we need to be tough—not mean, but firm in our approach and convictions. I respected and followed the rules and expected students and staff to do the same. I was mollified by his saying I was also "fair," a quality that seems a must in any leadership position.

Key ingredients that have impacted my life and leadership opportunities include the following:

- Respect for others in every situation. It won't always be returned, but that doesn't matter. Address the problem; don't attack the individual.

- Take every opportunity to learn (including applicable rules and regulations) and to grow skills across a broad spectrum.

- Be an active and engaged listener. ("The most important thing in communication is hearing what isn't said." –Peter Drucker)

- Always consider the *needs* of others.

- Start meetings on time; be respectful of others' time! (So many meetings at NOVA started late with attendees wandering in saying, "The traffic is so bad." It is ALWAYS bad! Start the drive earlier!)

- Be present—both physically and mentally. (Unless meeting-related or an absolute emergency, being on your phone or laptop during a meeting is simply disrespectful!)

- Be a clear communicator. (State and restate, if necessary.)

- Be honest and truthful with yourself, as well. "Truth is like a vast tree, which yields more and more fruit, the more you nurture it." –M.K. Gandhi

- Be transparent and reliable.

- Think "big picture"—spend time anticipating and preventing problems (instead of wasting valuable time solving problems that should have been prevented). "A clever person solves a problem. A wise person avoids it." –Albert Einstein

- Be consistent in your decisions. (Nothing causes more confusion or possible liability than inconsistency.)

- Be accountable. "To err is human, to forgive divine" (Alexander Pope). Avoid playing the blame game and take responsibility if the error is yours.

- Build trust; value each staff member. Trust is earned, not demanded or "inherited."

- "Great minds discuss IDEAS. Average minds discuss EVENTS. Small minds discuss PEOPLE." –Eleanor Roosevelt

- Give staff the information and training they need and permission to do their jobs, then get out of the way!

- Continue to provide instruction, guidance, and support as needed or change occurs.

- Encourage all positions to learn from each other.

- Allow others to lead and, in the process, aid in their development.

- Provide opportunities for and focus on continuous personal and process improvement, both for individuals and as a team.

- Create and maintain thorough policies and procedures that all team members can access—a track to run on, not a historical document.

- Maximize use of IT—safely and securely.

- Examine and eliminate "bottlenecks."

- Crosstrain for continuity and the unexpected (key individual "hit by a bus" scenario).

- Eliminate duplication of effort.

- Complete as many processes as possible earlier than the deadlines require.

- Don't jump for the sake of change, but always be open to opportunities, especially when not looking for them.

- Consider first the possible consequences of each of your decisions, short-term and long-range, but don't let fear paralyze decision-making.
- Never think you know it all or have all the answers. If you think you are the smartest person in the room, you are in the wrong room!
- Trust your colleagues until/unless they prove you can't.
- Ask to be part of the discussion if you aren't already.
- Make time for staff to have fun together and build community.
- Develop methods to reduce stress:
  - Take walks in nature.
  - Listen to the ocean or a stream and let it pull the stress right out of you.
  - Exercise/do yoga/tai chi.
  - Listen to peaceful music.
  - Get plenty of sleep.
  - Take short breaks.
  - Plan regular silent time. (Anne LeClair's *Listening Below the Noise* was the basis for a Silent Retreat my daughter hosted in the mountains of Colorado ... so healing and centering, though I confess that I talked to a chipmunk and a deer while on a walk!)
  - Breathe, just breathe.
- Be brave! Be bold ... no lifetime of "what ifs."
- Success is not the result of confidence. Confidence is the result of having success, and success is the result of preparation.
- You have one life to live. Live it well! There is no second turn on the merry-go-round. You are confined only by the walls you build yourself.

- "Go confidently in the direction of your dreams. Live the life you've imagined." –Henry David Thoreau
- Leave the party while you are still having a good time!
- No headlines!

Cowboy Code of the West:

- Know where to draw the line.
- When you make a promise, keep it!
- Be tough but fair.
- Live with courage.
- Talk less; say more. Listen!
- Always finish what you start.
- Remember, some things are not for sale (integrity, ethics ...).
- Do what has to be done.
- Take pride in your work.
- Ride for the brand.

A LETTER ON THE CAREER AND RETIREMENT OF JOAN ZANDERS, DIRECTOR OF FINANCIAL AID

August 12, 2021

As recently announced, Joan Zanders, NOVA's renowned director of financial aid, will retire August 31, 2021, after 13 years of highly commendable service at the college and an impressive 34-year career at various institutions at the level of director or higher.

Joan's education and career in the financial aid community began in Nebraska. She is a graduate of Midland Lutheran College in Fremont, Nebraska, and Wayne State College in Wayne, Nebraska, where she obtained her Master's in Education.

While working as a Financial Aid Director in Nebraska, she also served as president of the Nebraska Association of Student Financial Aid Administrators (NEASFAA) and as the president of the Rocky Mountain Association of Student Financial Aid Administrators (RMASFAA).

Upon moving to Virginia to become director of financial aid at NOVA in 2008, she continued her active involvement in the National Association of Financial Aid Administrators (NASFAA), serving as a board member, presenter, committee/task force member, and negotiator. She also assumed leadership roles in the Virginia Association of Student Financial Aid Administrators (VASFAA), where she served as VASFAA president from 2018 to 2019 and met many friends along the way.

As a respected financial aid administrator, Joan was often called upon at the national, regional, and state levels for her expertise. As one VCCS colleague recently joked, the feds would call her when they needed help understanding their own Dear Colleague letters and regulations.

Although Joan is adept at interpreting complex financial aid regulations, her true interests center more on influencing the future of financial aid. Over the years, she has met with federal and state lawmakers to help shape financial aid policies, and she has heavily invested her energy in developing NOVA's financial aid team.

Joan's goal was always for NOVA's Financial Aid Office to be the best in the country. While such statistics are not kept, Joan treats NOVA's financial aid team as if they are #1 in the country. Under Joan's leadership and direction, the financial aid department not only saw a significant improvement in financial aid operations but also a complete turnaround in the customer service provided to students. The number of FAFSA filers and aid recipients at NOVA more than doubled, and the amount of aid awarded each year increased from $33.7 million in 2007-2008 to approximately $120 million in more recent years. Joan implemented a lengthy process improvement plan that, in her own words, "Turned the Financial Aid Office Upside Down."

Key enhancements that Joan implemented at NOVA included:

- Setting up the Blackboard 24-Hour Student Support Center to reduce long lines, improve customer service, and provide a means for secure, electronic document submission
- Creating a centralized reporting structure that facilitated training and accountability
- Establishing and filling critical leadership positions in the Financial Aid Office

- Providing regular full-day Financial Aid-101 training sessions for staff in other departments
- Significantly increasing high school and community outreach
- Partnering with Inceptia to provide verification services, default prevention outreach, and financial literacy programs, the latter two of which helped NOVA's loan cohort default rate become among the lowest in the Virginia Community College System
- Implementing a financial aid fraud prevention program
- Contracting with FATV/Ocelot to provide students with access to an artificial intelligence chatbot, financial aid videos (including customized videos used for New Student Orientation), and an improved Satisfactory Academic Progress (SAP) appeal process
- Launched a Financial Aid Virtual Lobby

Joan, as you move on to your next adventure, the entire financial aid team at NOVA wishes you the very best! We are grateful for the profound impact you have had on our office, the college, and the entire financial aid community. It has been an honor and a true pleasure working with you! We leave you with one last bit of advice for your retirement, the same advice that you often gave us ... "No headlines!"

Joan Zanders

Submitted by:
Clint Young, Financial Aid, JCYoung@nvcc.edu

"YOU CAN'T GO HOME AGAIN"

According to Thomas Wolfe, "You can't go home again." If you expect it to be the same as when you left, Wolfe was certainly correct. There is a point in life when "someday" becomes "now."

After 41 years living outside of Iowa, including living in Montana, Nebraska, and Virginia, and saying goodbye to friends who will always remain dear friends, I returned to Iowa. Iowa has much to offer, including a lower cost of living and less traffic, but living closer to family was the goal.

At the time I moved, none of my immediate family lived east of the Mississippi River, though a grandson and his bride now do. Their wedding in historic Charleston, South Carolina, and an additional reception on Folly Beach were both beautiful and so much fun!

Moving from northern Virginia to a small town in Iowa has been an adjustment, to be sure, but I now get to see family more and have reconnected with friends from years gone by. I have thus far taken a hiatus from getting involved in the community, but I possibly will if or when I find a way to truly make a difference.

I now live in southwest Iowa, in what was considered the "city" when I was growing up seven miles from here. My community of 5,000 inhabitants is considerably larger than my little berg of 500 when I lived there and under 400 now.

My dad, who was the Superintendent of our truly outstanding reorganized school district for 22 years, would turn over in his grave to know that the school, which served three communities, is now closed due to fiscal mismanagement some 45-50 years after Dad left to become the head of the college in another community. Students who previously attended this school are now distributed to at least three different school districts in the larger surrounding towns.

Leadership requires anticipating change and creating and balancing budgets due to those changes. Some leaders think everything will simply continue as before. I have even experienced leaders who built in annual growth when all the statistics indicated otherwise. "If you always do what you've always done, you will always get what you have always gotten"—unless everything around you is changing, and you are not. Stated differently, "Insanity is doing the same things over and over and expecting different results."

I have seen so many vacant school buildings deteriorating into rubble, especially in formerly thriving small communities. Thankfully, my nephew and his wife have now turned the school building in my hometown into apartments and a beautiful wedding venue, which has helped maintain some population and activity.

The school population in rural America has been greatly impacted by the ever-increasing size of farms. Where there used to be a house with several children about every quarter section, one can drive for miles on many rural roads without finding a farmhouse. Farmhouses are now largely beautiful modern homes, not the farmhouses of yore, and with few or no children.

Land sells for thousands of dollars per acre, and farming is really big business. Just try buying a tractor or combine! The number of plants per acre can only be supported by more and more fertilizers, herbicides, and pesticides—all of which, unfortunately, run off into the water supply or float on the wind.

The Iowa Cancer Registry reported that Iowa had the second-highest and fastest-growing cancer rate in the nation in 2024. Community listening sessions are underway across the state, and legislation is needed to curb controllable factors.

According to Art Cullen, a columnist from Storm Lake, the gigantic elephant in the room is that Iowa has become a sacrifice state for cheap food and fuel. Probable carcinogens associated with industrial agriculture, including both plant and animal production, have increased steadily since 1990. Liberals and conservatives all want clean air and water, but when it's about money, don't expect those making the money to acquiesce.

My family has been greatly affected by cancer. One might think "genetically predisposed," but I can count at least six different types of cancer. My sister-in-law, who lost her husband/my brother to cancer 15 years ago, recently commented that she couldn't understand how so many entities were spending so much on cancer research, but no one was really finding a cure. It occurred to me that the answer lies in prevention, not a cure.

Simultaneously, I realized that there is no money in prevention—nor in some cures! The money is in pharmaceuticals, health insurance, the medical profession, farm chemicals, and on and on! Unless the populace says, "Enough!" and somehow provides money for prevention, big business will never put forth money to take away their profits.

Though much has changed in those 41 years away from Iowa, much has not. No matter where I live, human needs are much the same. We each deserve to be treated with respect and encouraged to continue learning and growing for better lives.

As a society and world community, we can—and MUST—do better! Everyone starts somewhere. How incredible it would be if we all had a common vision:

- To work for the greater good, and
- "To make this world a better place for our having been here."

Live, learn … lead!

From *The Velveteen Rabbit* on becoming Real: "Generally, by the time you are Real, most of your hair has been loved off, and your eyes drop out, and you get loose in the joints and very shabby. But these things don't matter at all because once you are Real, you can't be ugly except to people who don't understand … You become. It takes a long time. That's why it doesn't happen often to people who break easily, or have sharp edges, or who have to be carefully kept."[24]

---

[24] Rose Reed, Christopher Santoro, and Margery Williams Bianco, *The Velveteen Rabbit* (New York: Western Pub. Co, 1990).

MORE MEMORABLE QUOTATIONS ON LEADERSHIP

As you might have guessed, I have long been a collector of quotes, those little bits of wisdom in a sentence or two that speak volumes. Here are a few more:

"Two roads diverged in a wood, and I took the one less traveled by, and that has made all the difference." –Robert Frost

"If your dreams don't scare you, they are not big enough." –Ellen Johnson Sirleaf

"All it takes for evil to triumph is for good people to do nothing." –Edmund Burke

"Grit is that extra something that separates the most successful people from the rest. It's the passion, perseverance, and stamina that we must channel in order to stick with our dreams until they become a reality." –Travis Bradbury

"There is nothing so useless as doing efficiently that which should not be done at all." –Peter Drucker

"When we face the things that we fear, they no longer have power over us." –Ken Pett

"If you want to be a grown-up, you need to be your own hero." (author unknown)

"If you want to hire great people and have them stay working for you, you have to let them make a lot of decisions and you have to run by ideas, not hierarchy. The best ideas have to win; otherwise, good people don't stay." –Steve Jobs

"Leadership courses can only teach skills. They can't teach character or vision, and indeed they don't even try. Developing character and vision is the way leaders invent themselves." –Warren Bennis, *On Becoming a Leader*

"Remember not only to say the right thing in the right place, but far more difficult still, to leave unsaid the wrong thing at the tempting moment." –Benjamin Franklin (U.S. author, diplomat, inventor, physicist, politician, and printer [1706-1790])

"If virtue is not equal to power, power will be misused." –T. M. Alexander

"Never doubt that a small group of committed, thoughtful people can change the world. Indeed, it is the only thing that ever has." –Margaret Mead

"You must be the change you wish to see in the world." –M. Gandhi

"We are the ones we have been waiting for." –Barack Obama

"Whatever your mountain, climb on!" (anonymous)

"We do not inherit the Earth from our ancestors; we borrow it from our children." (Native American Proverb)

"When someone shows you who he is, believe him." –Maya Angelou

"Nearly all men can stand adversity, but if you want to test a man's character, give him power." –Abraham Lincoln

"We must rise above prejudice and beyond vengeance. If a spark is allowed to set the keg afire, the result will be a senseless tragedy of ignorant against ignorant,

injustice answering injustice—a holocaust that will drag down the innocent and right-thinking masses of human beings. (Then, we will all pay for not having cried for justice long ago.)" –John Howard Griffin, 1960—or now

According to a Gallup article by Marcel Schwantes entitled, "How Can You Be Sure Someone Has Great Leadership Skills? It *(Leadership)* Comes Down to This 7-Letter Word," Aretha Franklin voiced it clearly!—"All I'm Askin' for Is a Little Respect." Respect certainly must be part of every relationship.

During his eulogy for Jimmy Carter on January 9, 2025, Andrew Young, former U.N. Ambassador, used the following quote, which I believe he credited to Martin Luther King Jr.: *"To be a strong leader, one must have an antithesis in character—a tough mind and a kind heart."* Ambassador Young continued his tribute by saying, "James Earl Carter symbolized the greatness of this country."

"The soul of America is embodied in the sacred proposition that we're all created equal in the image of God. That was the sacred proposition for which Dr. King gave his life. It was a sacred proposition rooted in Scripture and enshrined in the Declaration of Independence. A sacred proposition [Dr. King] invoked on that day in 1963 when he told my generation about his dream—a dream in which we're all entitled to be treated with dignity and respect. A dream in which we all deserve liberty and justice. And it is still the task of our time to make that dream a reality, because it's not there yet." –President Joseph Biden, from **remarks** honoring Dr. Martin Luther King Jr. at Ebenezer Baptist Church in Atlanta (1/16/22).

"[I] think the greatest measure of strength of any individual is revealed based not on who you beat down but based on who you lift up. If you ever question your reason for being, what is your purpose, whether it matters, the answer will come when you realize the impact you can have on another human being, by everything from a kind word to doing what you all have been doing [here today]. [I]t's an extraordinary sign of the strength that we each possess and,

when we do it as a community, the impact that we can have on our world."
–Vice President Kamala Harris, from **remarks** at the MLK Day of
Service (1/16/22).

"Only when it is really dark can you see the stars." –Kamala Harris, 2024
Concession Speech

In her essay "At Harvesttime," Maya Angelou writes, "Although nature
has proven season in and season out that if the thing that is planted
bears at all it will yield more of itself, there are those who seem certain
that if they plant tomato seeds, at harvest time they can reap onions."
Reflect on the types of seeds the world needs to be planted today.

"We find ourselves in a moment of extreme polarization, revitalized preju-
dices, and an inability to discuss opposing views and find common ground
under the banner of our shared experience. … Yes, people can come together.
But only if they show each other grace and allow themselves open commu-
nication. Democracy has flaws but can succeed through great compromise. It's
crucial to not just hear someone's views but actually listen to them. E. pluribus
unum. Out of many, one." –Amy K. Dacey, Executive Director, Sine
Institute, May 1, 2023, opening remarks from Uncommon Table, an
east coast program initiated by the Sine Institute of Policy and Politics
at American University and the Center for Security in Politics at UC
Berkeley, which brought together national security experts and 20
students from each of the three participating institutions to encourage
them to find shared unity.

I recently read an article by Claire Richmond, a woman who has suffered chronic body pain for years, to the point that her "own body was
a frightening stranger." She finally found a specialist who diagnosed her
condition as acute hepatic porphyria (AHP), a rare metabolic disorder
that produces chronic symptoms and acute attacks. She found a physical
therapist who understood firsthand how to work with her challenges. I
quote her article: "Goal setting is a sensitive topic for me, a competitive,

recovering capitalist. I used to be all about SMART (Specific, Measurable, Achievable, Relevant, and Time-Bound) goals, but anymore this approach feels ableist and defeating. Now, I adopt goals that are FUN (Flexible, Uplifting, and Numberless). I first read of this concept from disability advocate and author Emily Ladau. I'm measuring my worth based on how well I live my values, not on what I accomplish or achieve."[25]

"My idea of being a good manager is keeping the people who hate me away from those who are yet undecided." –Casey Stengel

"Someone has to do something, and it is just incredibly pathetic that it has to be us." –Jerry Garcia, Grateful Dead

Preamble to "If These Were My Last Words," by Gerald Baliles, 65th Governor of Virginia, 1986-1990, Chair of the National Governors Association, 8/9/1988-8/1/1989:

Governor Baliles always wanted to leave a message in his speeches, eulogies, and other public comments. At his funeral, he wanted to leave a special message for all of you entitled, "If These Were My Last Words," which he delivered at a Renaissance Weekend at Hilton Head over New Year's Eve, 1993-1994. Various attendees were given topics and a couple of hours to prepare for the delivery of the remarks that weekend. Governor Baliles was assigned the topic, "If These Were My Last Words." These were not meant to be private words. These were public words.

Recently, the Governor found a copy of his remarks from 25 years ago in his files and felt that, in light of today's environment, this was the message he wanted to leave behind.

---

[25] After years of chronic pain, my own body was a frightening Stranger • Iowa Capital Dispatch, accessed August 30, 2025, https://iowacapitaldispatch.com/2024/02/03/after-years-of-chronic-pain-my-own-body-was-a-frightening-stranger/.

Renaissance Weekend XV, New Year's 1993–1994, Hilton Head, South Carolina, The Honorable Gerald L. Baliles, "If These Were My Last Words":

I would charge those who remain
to remember
that life goes on, and they must go forward,
recalling Jefferson's admonition that the earth belongs to
the living,
that while we should remember our past, and learn from it,
we must not become prisoners of it.

I would charge those who remain
to make the diversity of our nation a source of strength
rather than a force for division.

I would charge those who remain
to keep our country always free and restless,
energetic, curious about our physical world and our inner
space,
committed to faith and families as well as fun and fortune,
to social development as well as economic progress.

I would urge those who remain
to remember
that the measure of a civilization is its degree of enlightenment,
its commitment to education,
the promotion of the arts,
the treatment of the less fortunate;
its seriousness of purpose
and yet its ability to laugh at its foibles and the ironies of life.

I would charge those who remain
to remember
that we are citizens of a culture as well as a country,

and that there are obligations that go with that status;
and that among those are the promotion of learning,
the preservation of democratic values,
and the protection of our people against violence and
discrimination.

I would charge those who remain
to remember
that learning comes more from listening than lecturing,
that there is a difference between discussing and demanding;
between reasoning and reacting.
For life is a license:
to be lived fully and forcefully;
to make a difference in the world of change that has so tele-
scoped time and distance
and blurred the distinction between information and
knowledge,
between words and wisdom.

So, I would charge those who remain
to embrace change, not fear it;
to take its measure,
determine its direction and understand its dimensions;
for change is constant and often chaotic;
but if it can be harnessed it can be shaped for the good of
humanity.

Finally,
I would charge those who remain
to remember
that a civilization must be civilized,
that civility must be cultivated,
for it is the social glue that holds the fabric of our society
together.

Kindness counts;
good manners can move mountains.
The power of passion and the forces of energy are always
with us
and are necessary elements of ideas and actions,
but it is reason that can guide that passion
and civility that can harness that energy for the public good.

So, if these were my last words,
I would remind those who remain behind,
that they still possess the gift of life,
the length of which is not guaranteed;
but then the measure of life is not in its length
but in the length of its shadow.

And if life can be poetry in motion,
then remember the wistful words of Robert Frost
in "Stopping by Woods on a Snowy Evening."
He wrote …
I have promises to keep
and miles to go before I sleep,
and miles to go before I sleep.

GLOSSARY OF ACRONYMS

ACCT—Association of Community College Trustees

AOET—Aids Orphans Education Trust

AVP—Alternatives to Violence Project

BIA— Bureau of Indian Affairs

DNR—Department of Natural Resources

HFHI—Habitat for Humanity International

LRA—Lord's Resistance Army

NDLI—National Defense Language Institute

NEASFAA— Nebraska Association of Student Financial Aid Administrators

NASFAA—National Association of Student Financial Aid Administrators

NOVA or NVCC—Northern Virginia Community College

OGT—Orphan Grain Train

PTSD—Post-Traumatic Stress Disorder

RMASFAA—Rocky Mountain Association of Student Financial Aid Administrators

SASFAA—Southern Association of Student Financial Aid Administrators

VASFAA—Virginia Association of Student Financial Aid Administrators

WASFAA—Western Association of Student Financial Aid Administrators

W4TW—Women for the World

ACKNOWLEDGMENTS

To recognize and thank the many individuals who have influenced my life and consequently this book risks unintentional omission. I will then limit acknowledgments to those directly involved in the book.

- My sister Jane, a retired reading teacher, who twice proofread and helped edit and clarify the original copy.

- My daughter Miekka, who also proofread the original copy, made suggestions, and put me in touch with Shanda Trofe of Transcendent Publishing, who had assisted Miekka in publishing her book, *Being With Dementia: A Soulful Approach*.

- My former colleague Sam, who suggested the book, read the draft, and confirmed that it had indeed fulfilled his original hopes; and Alex, who read the manuscript draft, affirmed its value, and requested the section on "Building Community."

- Shanda and Mary of Transcendent Publishing for their work in editing, formatting, and publishing this book. I would not have wanted to try this without you!

- Each and every colleague and friend who, when they learned I was writing a book, pushed me to get it finished so they could read it!

If I failed to thank you, take consolation in knowing that you will be the thought that wakes me up in the middle of the night!

ABOUT THE AUTHOR

By profession, Joan Zanders is an educator with over 34 years of experience as a Director of Financial Aid, having served in four-year private and four-year public schools, and two community colleges during that time.

Her profession and avocation have focused on her father's advice to make the world a better place for her having been here. Within three to four years of entering the profession, Zanders was elected to office in the Nebraska Association of Student Financial Aid Administrators. Serving as President at the state level led to serving on many committees at the regional level, including co-chairing the regional conference, and later becoming President for the eight-state Rocky Mountain Association of Student Financial Aid Administrators.

Twice, Zanders co-presented sessions for each of the eight state conferences within the region, once on Conflict Management and once on Diversity. At the national level, Zanders served on the NASFAA Board of Directors and on multiple committees, including an early multicultural concerns committee, and as chair of the NASFAA Leadership Development and Professional Advancement Committee and Conference.

In Virginia, Zanders chaired the VASFAA Conference, served as VAS-FAA President, and chaired the Southern Association of Student Financial Aid Administrators (SASFAA) Conference 2020, "Courage,

Compassion, Collegiality: A Survivor's Guide for Uncharted Waters," an appropriate title still today.

Zanders presented many times at all levels of the profession, for the State Department, the National Indian Education Conference, staffers on the Hill, the Advisory Committee, and the House Committee on Education and the Workforce, and served on the Program Integrity Negotiated Rulemaking Committee.

During the process of securing assistance for military men and women impacted by 9/11 and the ensuing military activity, she participated in roundtable discussions with Dupont Circle organizations in D.C., which helped develop post-9/11 VA benefits.

Zanders has received state, regional, and national awards for her participation and leadership in the profession. She has a master's degree in Higher Education Counseling, is a trained facilitator for Alternatives to Violence Project, and is a Gallup Certified Strengths Coach.